"Robby Gallaty shares about his powerful transformation through the work of Jesus Christ in his book *Recovered*. After struggling with years of addiction, Robby encountered the living Savior! He learned firsthand to seek God for his identity; to be disciplined in prayer and Bible study; and to surround himself with godly mentors and those who will hold him accountable. His story offers hope to those who are struggling with addiction and challenges those who have settled for mediocrity in their relationship with Jesus."

Stephen Kendrick and Alex Kendrick
Filmmakers, *War Room* and *Overcomer*

"*Recovered* is a fascinating, page turning story of the path to—and freedom from—drug addiction. But there is so much more. It's a book of hope and help, filled with practical insights in helping others follow Jesus Christ and grow in their knowledge of and obedience to Him—which is essential! Like Robby (whose teaching I have happily sat under), I have never gotten over the wonder of being saved. What you read will not only reignite your passion to introduce others to Jesus Christ and disciple them; it will show you how. This is a book I will heartily recommend to those whose loved ones are in the bondage of drug addiction and need to understand what's going on with them and within them!"

Kay Arthur
Author, International Teacher, and Cofounder and Brand Ambassador of Precept Ministries: Engaging people in 185 countries in 83 languages in relationship with God through knowing His Word

"You'll really love this book. Robby's story of meeting Jesus and being changed is a picture of what the love of God does for all of us."

Bob Goff
New York Times bestsell
Everybody Always

"This book reads like a novel. You can't help but feel that there are crazy things happening to a fictional character who you hope makes it. But what's striking is that it's real, a real story of a real person finding the power of real change. Bravo to Robby for the bravery it takes to share a story like this."

Jon Acuff
New York Times bestselling author of *Finish: Give Yourself the Gift of Done*

"This is an amazing book! Pastor Robby Gallaty openly shares his story and his battle with his addictions. His journey is real and honest. When he finally was able to turn his life and will completely over to Christ, his life dramatically changed. God continues to use him to help many with their struggles. This book is a must read!"

Pastor John Baker
Founder of Celebrate Recovery

"Robby's story epitomizes God's transformational grace! I can relate in so many ways. Robby's been very inspiring to me and many others on what happens when our daily, intentional focus is to live in God's will as opposed to our own. If you are battling, been affected, or know someone who's dealing with the disease of addiction—then *Recovered* is a must read!"

Jeff Jarrett
Hall of Fame Wrestler

"*Recovered* is a powerful read for anyone struggling with addiction and the desire to be free. As you turn the pages of this book, your shame will be lifted through Robby's depth and honesty as he shows you how to enter freedom through the power of Christ."

Darryl Strawberry
Four-time World Series champion and evangelist

RECOVERED

RECOVERED

HOW AN ACCIDENT, ALCOHOL, & ADDICTION LED ME TO GOD

ROBBY GALLATY | with Rob Suggs

B&H
PUBLISHING
NASHVILLE, TENNESSEE

Published by B&H Publishing Group
Nashville, Tennessee

Dewey Decimal Classification: 616.86
Subject Heading: DRUGS AND CRIME / DRUG ABUSE /
REGENERATION (CHRISTIANITY)

Cover design by Faceout Studio; Jeff Miller.
Cover silhouette by Cole Gorman/Bleststudios. Cover
texture and light images: Meet Monpara/EyeEm/getty
images; Vitaly Sosnovskiy/shutterstock; alexkar08/
shutterstock. Author bio photo by Joanna McVey.

1 2 3 4 5 6 7 • 23 22 21 20 19

To my dad, mom, and sister.
Thank you for never giving up on me.

ACKNOWLEDGMENTS

I'm eternally grateful that Christ came looking for me, the chief of sinners, when I wasn't looking for him on November 12, 2002. Everything that has happened since my conversion is a result of him working in me to work through me. One of the secrets to my Christian life is that I've never gotten over being saved. I still remember that at one time I was lost and now I have been found.

I am grateful to God for my parents, Bob and Margaret, and sister, Lori, for sticking by my side. You demonstrated grace to me in a way that displayed the kindness of God. I wouldn't be where I am today without your support and love.

I'm thankful for godly mentors throughout my life: David Platt, Jim Shaddix, Tony Merida, Tim LaFleur, Don Wilton, Mark Dever, and Reggie Ogea. You have always been there for me whenever I needed direction, spiritual insights, or biblical advice.

I am grateful for the team of guys God has assembled around me. I appreciate Tim LaFleur, Gus Hernandez, Collin Wood, Jeff Borton, Greg Wilton, Chris Swain, and Dylan Young for reading through the manuscript to strengthen the book. I could not have written this book without your encouragement. It truly is a joy to serve together in ministry.

RECOVERED

I am grateful for the three churches I've had the privilege of pastoring: Immanuel Baptist, Brainerd Baptist, and Long Hollow Baptist. You have spurred me on to be a better pastor and disciple of Christ. You have taken the challenge to "go make disciples" seriously. For that, I am thankful.

Finally, I could not have written this book without the support of my wife Kandi and our two boys, Rig and Ryder. You have lived the pages of this book with me. I can't wait to write more in the future together.

CONTENTS

FOREWORD

BY DAVID PLATT

What do you do when a six-foot-six, 290-pound thieving drug-dealing addict, trained to fight, is standing next to you on a Sunday morning in a church gathering? My thought is that you become that guy's friend as soon as possible!

I have never forgotten the day I met Robby Gallaty. I haven't forgotten the privilege of baptizing him, not only because of what a special day it was, but also because this six-foot-six 290-pound man slipped on his way down into the baptistry and fell straight toward me, causing water to splash over onto the choir like a wave pool out of control. I haven't forgotten weekly lunches at Mr. Wang's Chinese food where we would talk about God's Word. I haven't forgotten early mornings together on our knees, crying out to God in prayerful desperation. And I haven't forgotten countless memories serving Christ alongside him in the US and around the world.

Yet amidst all that, I haven't forgotten about Robby. I have never gotten over how God saved him. His story, which he shares in this book, is a story of God's grace in action, God's patience in practice, and God's glory on display. After reading it, I am compelled to pray for two particular groups of people.

One, I pray for countless other Robby Gallatys in the world. Men and women who struggle with addiction in various ways. Men and women who might think they are too far removed from God to ever return. Men and women who try and try and try to overcome the temptations of this world, but they can't seem to find victory. Robby's story is a reminder to every single person that victory is possible. But that victory only comes through a personal relationship with God through trust in Jesus. I pray that you will read this book if you struggle with addiction, if you feel like you're far from God, or if you feel like you just can't conquer the trials and temptations before you. I pray that you will read it and realize that God loves you so much that he will change your life for you. I pray that you will discover that new life can begin right now for you through trust in Jesus, the only One who has conquered every trial and temptation, and ultimately sin and death.

Second, I pray for countless men and women, family members and friends, pastors and church members, who have Robby Gallatys around them. I pray that our eyes will be open to see them, and that our hearts will be open to love them. To pray for them and with them. To walk alongside them with patience and compassion, pointing them continually to God's Word as the way to true life. To live for God's glory in others' lives by pouring God's grace into their lives.

In the end, I think that's the main theme of this book: grace. But not just grace in Robby's life. As I read this book, I was overwhelmed by God's grace in my life. Sure, my story is a lot different from Robby's in many ways; but at the core, it's essentially the same. I was a sinner running from God, just like Robby. And God came running after me, just like Robby. And the good news is—God runs after people like you, too. So I pray that regardless of who you are or what you've done, you would know: new life is available to you now and forever by the grace of Almighty God. So I am compelled to pray that you will know this grace and show this grace, soak in it in your life and spread it all across the world, so that more and more and more stories like this one might be written to the glory of the one true God.

Chapter 1

TWO LIVES

Saturday night. Bourbon Street. Dinner at Galatoire's.

If you've ever hung out in the legendary French Quarter of New Orleans, you may have heard of our favorite restaurant. The best French-Cajun cooking in the city.

It's February 2001. I'm enjoying my usual: lamb chops with peas, potatoes, and onions. That's my favorite. I eat everything but the green-rimmed pattern on the plate. Mom, Dad, and Lori are talking about the movie we're about to see. Seeing as many movies as we have, you tend to become an amateur critic.

Dinner and a movie has been our family's go-to weekend outing since I was a kid—I'm now twenty-four. We rotate between Galatoire's downtown, or maybe Tony Angelo's, if we're in the mood for Italian. Or Ralph & Kacoo's for traditional Cajun seafood. Seafood (any style) is always okay with me—breakfast, lunch, or dinner. My favorite is crawfish and crab omelets. But if Dad gets to choose, it's going to be Galatoire's, because they make him feel like a million bucks.

My dad is a solid working-class guy. He runs a body shop nearby in Chalmette. He fixes up cars, puts in long hours, and enjoys being pampered by waiters who know his name.

He's never been into hunting or fishing, and he doesn't play golf. His hobbies are family, blockbuster movies, and a fantastic meal.

We're about to see *Cast Away* with Tom Hanks. Everyone's excited, except Mom. As usual, she's not all that excited. The dinner/movie thing isn't really her scene, but she's here for Dad.

My mom grew up with a tough family situation, and she's content just to stay home, cook in her own kitchen, and have her husband and two children near her.

Dad's on his second and probably final margarita of the evening—a drink with dinner is ingrained in New Orleans culture, but he never overdoes it. No way Mom would allow that. Dad is grinning over my anticipation. "They say Tom Hanks's costar is a volleyball? Really?" I'm asking.

Lori says, "That's what my friend says. She cried when he lost the volleyball." That draws a snort from Dad. He's laughing, covering his mouth to keep from spitting out his salad right there on the table.

"I saw that!" I say. "One point."

Over the years, mostly when I was in high school, we've had a little family game: Wait until your opponents are chewing, then make them laugh. You get one point if any food had to be spit out, two points for any liquid out the nose. Lori is giggling. Mom is rolling her eyes.

"Please," Mom says. "You're a grown man, Robby. And I *still* can't take you anywhere."

That makes it even harder for Dad, whose face is turning red now as he tries to swallow that bite. Nothing makes you laugh like being told not to laugh. That's why you should *never* take too big a bite around my family.

By the way, if he chokes, theoretically, that's three points. As yet, nobody has ever choked. Just saying.

"So what do you plan to do with your life, Robby?" asks my mother, attempting to corral the scene into some semblance of adult conversation. "Will you try to take the test again?"

"I don't think so, Mom. I'm really kind of into—"

"Not bartending again, I hope. You can't make a career out of that."

"Sure I can, Mom."

At this point, I'm into the Rave party scene. I've tried a shot as a techno DJ and loved every second. When I'm into something, it's ninety to nothing. If the water looks good, I don't dip a toe. I dive in headfirst. At this point in my life—at pretty much every point in my life—I crave stimulation, and the crazy sensory overload of nightclubs gives me that. I'm the center of attention.

As for the test, well, a few months back I began a training course to become a stockbroker, urged on by my parents. I never was convinced this was my thing, but by all accounts I showed a lot of promise. I wore a coat and tie, came in every day, and had a slick trainer. I was preparing for what they call a Series 7 test. Supposedly nobody has ever failed a Series 7 after this particular trainer prepped them.

Mom and Dad were pretty pumped. The day of the test, they moved me into a shotgun double apartment, complete with a full set of furniture they bought for me and brought in. My parents are the best. They had a cake, congratulations banners, and were bursting with pride for their wonderful new stockbroker of a son—who had to come in and break it to them he'd failed that test.

I got a 68 out of 100, two points short of passing. Of course, Mom and Dad were crushed, but they still had high hopes—I had to grow up sometime, right? For them, that means a coat-and-tie fast-track job when the sun is out, instead of working in loud clubs until three in the morning.

My parents have specific hopes for me, but they'd do anything for us, for Lori and me. And we'd do anything for them.

The problem is, I've blown the test, and I don't plan to tell them why. I had it nailed until that last section, and then, well, I blew it. Crashed in flames. What happened there? The guys giving the test just couldn't figure it out. I knew, but nobody else was going to.

———

Mom and Dad pick up the bill at Galatoire's, as usual. That's another thing about these family nights—it's always on Mom and Dad. As a teenager, I actually brought dates on these evenings with my parents, because it meant a movie, terrific food, and unsurpassed entertainment watching my family interact. My dates always adored my parents—everybody did.

We drive home together, to the home where I grew up, and then I say good night. Hugs all around. "I love you, Mom. Love you, Dad. You too, Lori." I watch them in the rearview mirror as I drive away, and I realize I'm shifting into my alternate mode—there's Family Robby, and then there's Street Robby.

It's now 10:00 p.m. I park about a block from my favorite hot spot, the Metropolitan, my club of choice. I make sure my stash is firmly in my right pocket. The left is for money. Before I climb out of the car, I crush and snort a couple OxyContin 40s. By the time I wipe the evidence clean from the case, the buzz kicks in. I'm ready for the night to begin.

This, of course, is what ruined the final portion of my stockbroker test. But for Street Robby, it's a way of life.

I walk into the club with pounding subwoofers greeting my ears. Strobe lights flash quick images of familiar faces as I walk across the room.

"What's up, Robby?"

"Hey man!"

"You're lookin' good, brother!"

The regulars all know me. Fist-bumps and handshakes are extended as I make my way toward the bar. I'm fully aware this is a shadow family, the flip side of my real one. Unlike my true and permanent family, the faces here come and go; relationships don't go very deep. But it's still my world.

As a functioning addict, I'm able to hang out with my parents, and they never suspect a thing. I'm in full control. But in the clubs, there's nothing to hide. I can give in to my impulses, and nobody's going to judge me. Most are joining in with me.

"Robby!"

It's Ron, one of my acquaintances who buys drugs from me. His eyes gesture toward a door to a back room, and I follow him there. I yell into his ear, though with the music pounding, it sounds like a whisper.

"How many tonight?" I ask, reaching for my pocket.

He wants ten Oxys, twenty Ecstasy pills, and a few Somas. He'll turn it around in the club for a profit, which will support his habit for a few days. Unless he gives in and uses his stash before he can sell it. Which happens to him—and sadly, to me, if I don't sell it quick. Then the money's gone, and I owe more than I can sell.

I can tell something's on Ron's mind. He looks me in the eye and says, "Did you hear about G?" I shake my head, but I

5

know what's coming. It occurs to me I haven't seen G around for a week or so.

"Gone. Overdose. His roommate found him."

I take a deep breath and close my eyes for a moment. I don't have to be told the cause of death. I can't think of anything to say. What *could* be said? No words are right.

Ron breaks the silence. "We've got to get out of this, man. This whole thing."

"Yeah, I know. We'll do it. Been thinking about that myself. There has to be more to life than this."

"Yeah. Let's get together and talk soon."

"For real. This week."

We fist-bump and part ways, both knowing we're not "getting out of this." There is no escape hatch. Well, actually, there is one—G found it.

———

The next few hours are a blur. I know we end up in the French Quarter; I remember walking by Galatoire's, where the other Robby was a few hours ago. Sunday is kind of fuzzy, too, and then it's Monday and the phone is ringing. I pick it up. It's Mom. She sounds incredibly tense.

"Hi, Mom! What's going on?"

Her voice is ice cold. Mom has her own brand of ice cold. "Robby, we know. We know what you did."

"What I did? What are you—"

Suddenly it hits home, like a knife slicing into my heart. The absolute worst possible thing I can imagine. Of *course* they know. I dreaded this day would come. I wait, speechless for once.

"Fifteen thousand dollars, Robby. *Fifteen thousand.* How could you do this to us? We would have given you anything in the world, and you stole from us? Your father is so furious he—"

"Look, Mom, calm down. You don't understand. It's just . . ."

And that's all I've got. All out of words. How am I supposed to explain why I've run up thousands of dollars on their credit card—why I need money so desperately?

Back when I was working for him, Dad trusted me with his business credit card. I memorized the number. One day, a few months back, I needed something and was flat broke, and thought about that card. *Just this once.* Dad wouldn't mind. I'd pay him back.

But of course, I didn't. It was just a little too easy to give in to temptation and snort my own stash instead of selling it, knowing I could quickly convert that card to cash on the buy-and-pawn plan. Dad wouldn't notice, or so I told myself. He spent thousands of dollars each month, purchasing auto body parts for his business. He'll never notice the periodic charges on his statement. He never checks his statements closely.

I got so used to abusing that card that one night, when I saw a Fender Stratocaster online, I decided it was meant for me. All the great guitarists—Hendrix, Clapton, all of 'em—played Strats. I placed an order, throwing in a single stack Peavey amp. Then, a while later, the phone rang at Bob's Collision Center, my dad's shop. Somebody from the online store wanted Robert to know that his $600 guitar was on back order.

Was there some mistake? My dad was more than certain he hadn't ordered some expensive guitar.

Well, they said, your card was used for the transaction.

Mom and Dad began to study the last few credit card bills, and I was busted. It was like waking up from a bad dream into a full-fledged nightmare, because I realized the stupidity of thinking I could ever get away with something so dumb. I also realized, in the pit of my stomach, the terrible toll this would take on my parents' trust.

Mom says, quietly but firmly, "Don't ever come to our house again. We don't want to see you."

I spit out my reply in anger. "Well, I don't need either of you."

And we both hang up. I sit for an hour, trembling, thinking, *What have I done?*

For some time, my life has been spiraling wildly out of control, plunging downward. Now I've hit absolute bottom.

How did I get here?

Chapter 2

PLAYING PARTS

Chalmette lies just east of downtown New Orleans, in St. Bernard Parish. Chalmette means "pasture land" or "fallow land." When soil is fallow, that means it lies unsown, fertile, waiting for planting. Which is a picture of my life in those early years.

The town I remember from childhood was twice the size it is now. In 2005, Hurricane Katrina pushed the Gulf waters over and across our town, devastating it and changing it forever. Along with all the other residents, we lost everything in that storm. The Chalmette of those years exists only in our memories.

We were a typical working class family. Dad owned and operated his collision center, his life revolving around fixing up mangled cars. Mom worked for an oil and gas company. My sister and I went to school, played with neighborhood friends, and tried to stay out of trouble.

We were a religious family, or to be more exact, a church-based family—not particularly spiritual. As good Catholics of our parish, we attended Mass on Sundays and went to confession the following Saturday if we missed it. We weren't Christmas-and-Easter-only attenders, but still, churchgoing was a duty, and God was merely someone you visited for an hour once a week. He didn't involve himself in family life too much, at least not in ours. I never saw him as a God of love, but as an authority figure who was out to chastise me whenever I stepped out of line.

Speaking of me, well, you know that kid beloved by all adults, the teacher's pet, well-behaved and perfect in every way? Have you got a good mental picture of that child? Well, that's not me.

Look over to the other side of your mental picture. See that other kid, the one with the sneaky grin? The kid being glared at by the teachers? The class clown, who had to be talking and getting out of his desk no matter how often he was warned, no matter how many times he got into trouble? The class champion of time-outs?

Yeah, *that* one. That's me.

During the eighties, attention deficit disorder (ADD) and attention deficit hyperactivity disorder (ADHD) were first emerging as real issues of children's health. Although I wasn't formally diagnosed, everyone knew there was a problem. The doctor explained to my mom there were reasons I was out of control, reasons that could be managed through various options.

She suggested Ritalin, which inhibits those impulses, but my parents weren't comfortable with that strategy. Instead, they opted for the Feingold diet, a way of controlling behavior through meal choices. For years I couldn't eat anything with artificial flavors, preservatives, or colors. It's fair to say the diet had mixed results. I definitely wasn't an enthusiastic Feingold kid.

A plan was needed to avoid eating bland food. How do you convince your peers to trade you their lunch for the uninspiring Feingold diet choices that lay in my lunch box?

Well, you learn the art of salesmanship at an early age. These skills would come into play years later.

The broader lunch selections were great for enjoyment, but horrible for my behavior. My issues came to a head when I was in seventh grade. Miss Franklin stepped out of the classroom one day. Crawling under her desk, I seized an opportunity for entertaining my classmates. They were already starting to laugh, eager to see the next episode of the Robby clown show, when the teacher walked in. I froze under her desk. She sat in her chair about to roll into the desk. *Busted.*

"Mr. and Mrs. Gallaty, it's time to do something about Robby's behavior," declared the principal.

That was the end of my time at St. Mark's. My parents moved me to Holy Cross, a Catholic school for boys, where the Catholic brothers were armed with paddles and ready to strike at any time. They would chew up and spit out class clowns far worse than me, and I knew I'd fallen into desperate circumstances. I was utterly stifled.

Worse, I found myself in the middle of an academic enigma. I excelled on my entrance examinations, qualifying me for honors work. My parents were thrilled by this, of course, and so was I—until I realized it meant more studying. I hadn't read the fine print on this one. A trap!

So here I found myself in a highly regimented Catholic school with twice as much schoolwork and an unlimited supply of bottled up energy. It took me a full semester to get downgraded from Honors. By that time, I was entering eighth grade, a tough year for most kids to begin with. It was going to be even worse for me because I had no friends. The gifted crowd thought I must be a dunce because I hadn't made it in their group. The "regular" class thought I was a nerd, because I'd at first been lumped in with the smart kids.

The ultimate punishment for a class clown is to be an outcast, and of course, I was an outcast with deadly paddles threatening me at every moment with schoolyard work awaiting those who broke the rules. In short, I was in the midst of adolescence and not loving life.

By ninth grade I had managed to accumulate a grand total of two friends at Holy Cross, so I clung to them tightly. One of them was named Keith. I remember him passing on at recess what he felt to be one of the great secrets of the universe. "Robby," he said, "there are two types of people in this world: those who listen to Jimi Hendrix, and those who *hear* Jimi Hendrix."

"Wow," I said, "that's deep." It sounded like he was really onto something. He gave me further instructions to intensify the experience: "Turn up the volume, burn some incense, and lie on your back to take in the music."

I convinced Mom and Dad to drive me to the French Market downtown to purchase incense to accompany my musical endeavor of "hearing" Jimi Hendrix. For obvious reasons, they weren't as eager as I was, but they complied.

Even with patchouli incense sticks burning in my bedroom as *Are You Experienced?* by Hendrix blared from my stereo, I didn't exactly take in the effects that were promised. Keith, I'd later discover, had forgotten to mention one crucial ingredient: smoking marijuana apparently aided his kind of "hearing."

The whole Jimi Hendrix experience didn't seem to work out, but I had discovered my own kind of secret of the universe: There were those who listened to schoolteachers, and those who *heard* them. I *listened*, not so much to learn what they were teaching, but to pick up their speech patterns and pet phrases. I developed a knack for impersonating most of the faculty. I'd take close notes of not Mr. Frederick's physics lectures, but of Mr. Frederick *himself*, picking up on all his little affectations. Then, in the lunchroom, I'd do a spot-on impersonation.

The students loved it. Once again, the class clown was back performing, and I'd found an identity. No longer a nobody, I was "that guy who does impressions of all the teachers."

If Mr. Frederick wasn't getting laughs, then just like that I could become Mr. Pineda from the religion department or Mr. Rung, my history teacher. I could be anyone. It didn't matter, as long as heads were turning my way. As long as the laughter kept flowing. As long as the attention was coming toward me, demanding more and more stimulation.

The time would come years later, in therapy, when a counselor would point out to me that this was a highly significant moment. I was playing parts, trying to be someone I wasn't. I'd continue performing for a number of years and in a number of ways. There was an emptiness at my core—I had no idea who I was—so I could only feel comfortable when I was "being" someone else.

Maybe Keith would have put it this way: The world was made up of those who *played* real people . . . and those who *were* real people.

Chapter 3

JUST LIKE MAGIC

You've probably heard about New Orleans during Mardi Gras. Yes, it's a wild way to bring in the springtime. Mardi Gras is a festival held for a couple of weeks leading up to "Fat Tuesday," the beginning of Lent. With parades every day, it's basically one long, citywide party.

If you're a sixteen-year-old New Orleans male, addicted to activity and stimulation, then you're right in the middle of the action. There's color, noise, music, and, of course, more than a little alcohol.

I began drinking moderately the year I turned sixteen, something absolutely normal in Louisiana culture. It's a bit like England or Germany; alcohol is a part of every social gathering. It wasn't out of character for me to go to a bar with my fake ID, order a Bloody Mary, and then suit up to play a basketball game for my school.

So my buddy Chris and I were in the French Quarter waiting for the Bacchus parade. It's one of the highlights of Mardi Gras, held on the Sunday before Fat Tuesday with amazing floats and national celebrities. I walked into Jax Brewery, a historic site that is now more like a shopping and restaurant mall. A little crowd was gathering over to the side, and at the center of it, there was a man performing magic tricks.

I'd seen magic tricks performed on television before, but never in person. This shouldn't have been any turning point in my life, except it was. My path was about to take a slight but meaningful twist.

I was a sophisticated, worldly-wise junior in high school, right? I rolled my eyes at this little demonstration and the crowd of spectators hanging onto every move. *What adult does magic tricks?* I thought. *Nothing but kid stuff.*

Yet that crowd kept growing. As a veteran class clown, I had a healthy respect for anybody who could command attention, however they did it. I couldn't help but watch, and suddenly the magician was looking right back at me. "Hey, big man, come here," he said. "I need your help on this next trick."

Who, me? I looked right and left, but there were no other "big men" around; I was well on my way to six and a half feet tall.

"Yeah, you!" he said. "Come on, let's go!

I left Chris, walked to his side, and the magician said, "Here's your job. Guess how I do this trick, and you *don't* have to buy it."

Laughter from the crowd—so *that* was it. He was selling something. But before I could open my mouth to object, he pulled out a silk cloth, poked it into his left fist, and—hold it, where did it go? He reached over and pulled it across my top button and out of my shirt top pocket. Before I could catch myself, I gasped.

"Did you catch it? How did I do it?"

"Um—"

Laughter again. I was utterly stumped. I hung around until he was finished, trying to figure out at least one of his tricks. I had struck out and stood looking at him sheepishly. He offered his right hand and said, "Jeff Schmidt."

"Robby Gallaty." I introduced my friend as well.

"I'm just in from Vegas, Robby—new here, but what do you say we go grab a bite to eat? It's on me."

We walked down Decatur Street and had a couple of beers, and Jeff performed tricks all night. Watching the parade was an afterthought at this time.

I could see this was his style; he became the center of attention everywhere he showed up, because magic tricks are so compelling. Who else challenges you to watch with such complete attention? A magician says, "I'm going to fool you, and I *dare* you to catch me at it!"

Supreme command of a room was something I could get behind. Besides, Jeff had a couple of really cute waitresses practically eating out of his hand. He threw cards on the ceiling, and they'd stick there like glue. He tore cards in twos and threes, and just like that, they were in one piece again. We were all spellbound.

Jeff looked over at us, saw our eyes bulging, and laughed. "Tell you what," he said. "One trick I *can't* do is make a vehicle appear. You guys drive me around town, and I'll teach you how to do the tricks you've seen. Deal?"

We looked at each other, already nodding yes. We *had* to learn those secrets.

I say *we*, but I was the one who proved to be his star pupil. I wasted no time incorporating magic tricks into my lifestyle. Before long, I was running for student body president at my high school, putting on magic shows to get votes.

I added my own brand of humor and presentation, and it was a nice fit.

Magic was my new thing, meaning, my new *obsession*. As I've said, if I did something, I did it all out. I became pretty good at these illusions, and over the years I found they'd open all kinds of doors, including (*particularly* including) preaching opportunities. But during my junior year of high school, that particular door wasn't one that would even occur to me.

For now, I wanted to entertain my friends and impress girls. If somebody upstairs was watching out for me, lining up everything that would point my life to a certain destination, I was none the wiser.

When I wasn't making scarves appear and disappear, I was playing basketball or guitar. With my height and intensity, I began to stand out on the court. My parents never missed a single game. They were proud of me as I began putting up points and making all-star teams. In particular, they were thrilled that basketball gave me an opportunity to have a fully paid college education. Some of the smaller colleges were scouting me, and I eventually committed to attend the University of North Carolina at Greensboro. North Carolina is a state known for its university system (not to mention its basketball), and this was a great opportunity.

The only problem was that Greensboro was eleven hours away. When I was a senior, there was a girlfriend in the picture. Isn't there always?

I'd been dating her for almost a year, and naturally, she was way up on my priority list. She was headed to LSU, nearby in Baton Rouge. I wasn't interested in North Carolina girls—*this* was the only one who counted. She confronted me, "Robby, you can't go that far away! Can't you find somewhere a little closer to home?" And you know, when your girlfriend says it to you, in just the right tone of voice, you're likely to do almost anything.

I began to think about nearby colleges that had basketball programs. It was very late in the recruiting game, of course; the important schools had filled out their rosters. But I figured a Division I prospect like me could get some interest from a smaller NAIA program. I got out the phone book and called William Carey College in Hattiesburg, Mississippi—a simple ninety-minute drive. I didn't know a great deal about Carey, just that it had a basketball team and wasn't far from my girlfriend. I called the head coach and told him my situation. He hesitantly agreed to look at me in a tryout session—the team was already set.

"You're too impulsive," said my mom as she drove me up to Carey.

"Impulsive, but also close to home, if this works out," I pointed out. She had to admit she didn't mind that idea. Eleven hours away, and my parents would see me only for summer and Christmas, only making it to a couple games in person.

Something strange happened at the tryout: I played well—that is, I played *really, really* well. As if the spirit of Michael Jordan got into me for an hour. Afterward, Mom said, "I've seen every basketball game you've played, and a lot of the practices, and you've never played like that—ever. You must really like this girl!"

I shrugged. Again, it just felt like something that worked out. Just like magic.

When you're young, you expect things to fall neatly into place. As you get older, you may begin to feel there are higher purposes at work. Some might even call it divine providence. In my seventeen-year-old mind, I thought it was all about a girl, but now I see other things were moving into place.

Coach was all smiles. It didn't take him long to offer me a scholarship to play for the William Carey Crusaders. I called UNC-Greensboro and let them know I had a change of plans.

One simple, impulsive decision had vast implications. The irony was that two weeks after school started, my girlfriend broke up with me—having gotten the mistaken idea that I was cheating on her. Her reasoning was that I wanted to purchase clothes at the mall, something I hadn't done before. If I'd wanted to cheat on her, I'd have gone eleven hours away! She was the whole reason I was here playing for an NAIA school instead of one that could be invited to March Madness.

But I took stock of my new home—a very *Baptist* new home.

My entire culture growing up was so thoroughly Catholic, I didn't even *know* a Southern Baptist, and now I was surrounded by a whole army of them.

William Carey is named after the Father of Modern Missions, who lived in the eighteenth century. I was in a whole new subculture. There was no casual drinking. No Thursday night Frat parties. Faith was more overt, and I found myself to be the number one target of a campus game called "Convert the Catholic."

I made a visible target, cruising through the campus in my red 944 Porsche, blaring uncensored Tupac tracks from the ten-inch bazooka subwoofers in my trunk. I always had a nice car because of my dad's occupation. He'd told me that if I could maintain a B average and earn a college scholarship, he'd fix up any car I'd wanted to drive, other than a Ferrari or a Lamborghini. He forgot to mention Porsche, so that was my choice. He fixed one up and made it look brand-new.

I had brought my rap music, my alcohol, my sports car, and especially my Roman Catholic affiliation to this new

Baptist world. For the first time, I knew what it was like to hold down first place on every local prayer list. Or to be a deer during hunting season.

I'd be walking to campus, and a vague acquaintance would approach me. "Hey, Robby! Wait up!" I could see the Bible and the tract in his hand.

"Hey, man. What's up?"

"How's basketball going?"

"I'm redshirting this year. Waiting on the six-foot-six and six-foot-ten guys to graduate."

"Cool. Hey, if you were to die tonight, do you know where you'd—"

"Good talk, man, but I'm going to be late for class."

I'd duck into a doorway—didn't matter which doorway—and escape another barrage of earnest gospel invitations. I couldn't understand this whole witnessing culture. All these people hardly knew my name, but they were intent on asking me to walk away from how I was raised and take on their form of religion. Catholics didn't operate like this; you were born into it or you weren't. When people asked me if I was a Christian, my go-to response was, "I'm Catholic." End of story.

But I liked the school, and being the evangelism target didn't put me off too much. I simply avoided it and lived my life.

Except for Jeremy Brown. He was the asterisk in the big conversion quest. Jeremy had a whole different approach to sharing his faith with me, and amazingly, he was the only one who seemed to have figured out the right formula. He offered friendship instead of an evangelistic sales pitch. Jeremy took the time to get to know me and let me get to know him, just the way any college buddy would. He cared about me rather than my religious scalp.

Jeremy loved playing the guitar, just like I did. He enjoyed all kinds of music and introduced me to Christian rock, which surprisingly turned out to be pretty good. Jeremy could look me right in the eye—literally. He was six-five, and I was six-six. Not to mention that both of us grew up in Louisiana. And occasionally, he would mention some aspect of his faith, not as a weapon aimed at me, but as a part of the whole world of Jeremy Brown—a world where I enjoyed hanging out. It made his faith intriguing instead of annoying. It was contagious.

I had no intention of enlisting in the William Carey Baptist army, but my defenses were worn down, and I actually found myself playing in a Christian rock band. I guess we had nothing better to do. Jeremy played rhythm, I handled lead guitar, and we had two vocalists and a drummer.

Christian rock was now my jam—not the beliefs, just the tunes. As a matter of fact, we'd have jam sessions late at night in my dorm room until someone would call security. The guard would come knocking at the door to tell us to turn off the amps and go to sleep. Of course, the guys would be hiding under my bed by this time. I'd put on my robe, shut the lights off, mess up my hair, go to the door, and innocently tell the guard, "It wasn't us, sir. We were trying to sleep, but we hear it, too. Hope you can find out who's doing this."

He'd shake his head and walk away, while we plugged back in to lay down a few more riffs.

The band was just for kicks, except for my tendency to go over the top. After two months of practicing, I went to the college president and asked him if we could play at Carey Fest, where various Christian bands were invited to perform. The idea was, why not have the school's own band represented?

He agreed, and I went back to share the good news with the band.

"You did what?" asked the drummer. "We've never played in public!"

Jeremy said, "Robby, what name did you give them? Because we don't *have* one."

"Oh, yeah. Guys, we're officially the band *Nothing Better to Do*. Because, you know, that's what we've got."

A couple of them rolled their eyes.

I think it worried Jeremy that his Christian band was fronted by a non-Christian, and it was about this time he decided to sit down with me and take the next step in sharing his faith. He had earned the right to speak, because he was my best friend. So I listened.

"I know you don't have a deep, daily faith in Jesus Christ," he said. "You were raised in the church and taught about Jesus, but that's not exactly saving faith. There has to be a time when you go from death to life. It's absolutely necessary for eternal life. It's all about saying 'yes' to him with everything you are. Not to mention you avoid hell by going to heaven when you die."

"I get that," I said. "But I was christened as a baby."

"Sure, but Jesus wants to have a real *relationship* with you—not just something your parents did when you were too young to understand. Saving faith comes from the heart. You and I are friends because we *chose* it. That's why it's a real friendship, something we live out every day. Friendship is active and real. So is a saving faith in Jesus."

"I get that, too. It makes sense. But how do you do it exactly?"

"If this is something you really want, Robby, if you understand that sin is a part of your life, and you can't handle it alone, you can cry out to the Lord through repentance and faith. All you need to do is pray a simple prayer, like the one I'll give you, and mean every word. Robby, do you think you're ready to pray that kind of prayer with me?"

"Sure."

"You're really sure about this? It's serious, man."

"Yeah, I'm sure."

He prayed, leaving spaces after each phrase for me to repeat. I acknowledged my sin before God, my need for his forgiveness, and asked Jesus to save me. Afterward, he gave me a big hug and welcomed me into God's kingdom.

And for several days, I figured I was just like Jeremy and all the "Carey Christians" now. He led me along, took me to church, and I did all the things I felt I was supposed to do. But for me, as a musician, it was like playing a song I didn't know, just chord by chord from a chart, without feeling the melody. I have to feel the song *inside*, and I didn't feel this form of faith inside me. I'd said a prayer on the basis of not wanting to go to hell, without understanding there needs to be a deeper, more personal and desperate desire. I needed to feel the weight of my sin and the need for salvation.

What I lacked was something greater than "magic"—the supernatural effect, the transformation of new birth. My commitment wouldn't last, and in time I would understand that the test of real faith is fruit.

Jesus said you tell a tree by what it produces, and what came out of my life wasn't the fruit of godliness. I was a good kid from a good family, but still lost as lost could be.

Yet the seeds had been planted for that tree of eternal fruit. Someday the seeds would sink into the soil, and the real transformation would come. Just like magic.

For now, all I could see was the illusion.

Chapter 4

BIZ WHIZ

On college campuses, the weekend begins on Thursday. Even in Southern Mississippi. Even at a Baptist college. I may have played in a Christian band in 1995, but I was partying like it was 1999.

I had a red Porsche, a tendency to drink, a crowd-pleasing magic act, and a love of fun and excitement. In retrospect, my college basketball career never stood a chance.

In high school, I was used to being *the* big guy at six-foot-six. In college ball, even at an NAIA school, there were taller towers. Some of our guys were six-ten and six-eleven, so I couldn't just park under the basket, wait for a pass, and take my shot. I actually had to learn to move the ball in traffic, including dribbling.

Don't laugh—dribbling may sound pretty basic, but at a higher level of ball, against gifted athletes, it's not a given, even with my work ethic.

The coach expected a big return on a Division I scholarship guy like me. He was in my face, pushing me harder than I'd ever been pushed as an athlete. After a while, as I struggled, my longtime love for basketball began to cool off.

Still, I had a campus jock image to maintain. My room-mate played baseball, and I knew he dipped snuff. But on my birthday, September 20, he said, "Hey, I think I'll pick up a pack of cigs."

"I didn't know you smoked," I said.

"Just on special occasions. And tonight is a special night."

I had never smoked before, but college is all about figuring out how adulthood should look. I well knew that my grandfather, Mom's dad, died from smoking. He was so addicted at the end of his life, he tried getting workers to smuggle cigarettes into the nursing home while he was on oxygen. I told myself I was only going to smoke on special occasions, such as a birthday.

And a little later, weekends. For me, they were special occasions, right?

And a little after that, I threw in Thursdays. Like I said, they're part of the weekend on campus.

Then, what the heck, Monday needed to be a smoking day, too, because that's when Monday night football happens.

After that, I was a full-blown smoker. Why not consider life a special occasion? I brought my several-pack-a-day habit home for the summer, when I sold cars to pick up some extra cash. When you're in college, summertime is a special—well, you get the idea.

When I came back to Hattiesburg in September, I was a chain-smoking, coffee-guzzling, six foot-six inches of *out-of-shape*. I came off the court wheezing after cross-court fast breaks, with the coaches glaring at me. What should have been a productive off-season turned out to be a nightmare when school started back.

One day I was late to practice (again). I caught the usual verbal abuse and was told to start running. With every huffing, puffing step, I came closer to the boiling point. I hadn't come to South Mississippi to run up and down the steps of the gym. An assistant coach, who wasn't my biggest fan in the first place, made a choice remark to me as I loped by. I tossed an even choicer remark right back—not cool for scholarship players who are underperforming. Earn a starter spot, or at least make the squad, and maybe you attain a few sarcasm privileges. Me, not so much. None of this stopped me from firing back, and smoke started coming out of the assistant coach's ears. He snapped, "Go upstairs and change! You're out of here."

Everybody on the team turned my way.

I responded with another smart-alecky comment, went upstairs to grab my gear, hung my Nike team shoes around my neck, and headed for the door.

"Leave those shoes, Gallaty!" the coach shouted. They were team property.

I whirled around. "Come and get 'em!"

As he walked toward me, I reached back as far as I could and launched them over his head toward the back wall. "They're all yours, *Coach*."

I knew now I'd burned this bridge to the ground. I crossed the point of no return. This wasn't one of those little storms that would blow over in a couple of days. I was dispensable to William Carey basketball. There would be no coming back now, no cooling-off period followed by a "let's put this behind us" handshake.

Oddly enough, my college basketball career lasted a season and a half; smoking lasted nine years.

I wasn't one to look back. I still had a lot going on, and maybe now, an extra edge—a touch of attitude. I was invited to every party. They'd be waiting for me when I made an entrance with my briefcase of card tricks, scarves, and illusions. Most drinks were purchased by others as compensation for the tricks. I was the man of the hour, and all of it was a recipe for disaster.

Sure enough, I was pulled over in traffic by the police one night, coming from a party. I had taken advantage of more than a few free drinks. Swerving red sports cars aren't overlooked by the state police.

I parked my Porsche on the shoulder close by my school, stood beside it, and went through field sobriety tests. (Little did I know, my wheels would be taken away from me after this semester for finishing with a 1.9 GPA.)

Meanwhile, my buddies were driving by in their own cars, honking and waving. I waved back, grinning each time. The officer looked up at me and said, "You wave at one more car and you're headed for the backseat of my cruiser—then to the station, where I'll book you."

"Yes sir," I said, and focused on pulling myself together.

He gave me a closer look and said, "Are you a Christian, son?"

Where did that come from? I followed his eyes to the cross I was wearing. "Yes, sir, I am," I said.

"Well, I'm going to give you a warning. Just this once. But don't ever drive again if you've been drinking. You understand what I'm saying?"

"Yes sir."

"Now you call a friend to come drive you home. Got it?"

"Yes sir. Thank you, sir."

I began to think about how my parents would react if I got a DUI. I'd somehow dodged a bullet. As I sat down behind the wheel and watched the officer drive away, I told myself it was time to clean up my act. Basketball was gone—good riddance—but I needed to cut out the foolishness. This wasn't the way I'd been raised.

I gathered my resolve and walked the straight path—for a whole day or two. Then, as always, my newfound determination faded, like me trying to run a fast break. I was morally out of shape, and I was more interested in trying on identities: jock, Christian rock star, magician, life of the party, whatever anyone was looking for.

And now, a new one: I was trying on the mask of the business whiz—the ultimate symbol of adulthood.

———

I was invited by my roommate to attend a PBR—Public Business Reception—for a company called American Communications Network. The line the spokesman gave me would be one I would perfect: "If the money were right and it fit into your time schedule, would you be open to looking at a serious business opportunity?" Who could say no to that?

This was a multi-level marketing organization, a telecommunications company looking for young people who were energetic, aggressive, and needed money. That was me. So Dad and I attended the meeting and listened to their pitch. "You can sell long distance service," the spokesman said. "We give you the opportunity to build your own business and make thousands of dollars while working part-time. The only limit to your success is in the time and passion you bring to it. We have young adults buying new cars, touring Europe, or financing grad school."

I looked at Dad. I no longer had a scholarship paid for by the athletic department, and I needed some way to fund tuition and books, not to mention providing spending money. All ACN wanted was a $500 registration fee, but I didn't have it. Dad said, "If I put up the money, that's my part of the deal. Your part is to work my contacts the way they describe it. Are you willing to do that?"

"I'm in!" And I was—I was all in.

I worked the phones zealously. It turned out I had a knack for sales. The idea of ACN was to sell the product first, then the company itself. You looked for promising phone users and converted them to sellers like yourself. Then they'd be part of your "downline," and you'd pick up a commission on all their sales. In turn, they'd build their own downlines.

I lived on the telephone, especially during the summer when I would sell cars by day and work ACN by night. As competitive as I was, this was the kind of arrangement that motivated me. Network marketing has a powerful attraction because of the idea of exponential growth.

The company set out benchmarks to shoot for, "levels" to climb. I hit the first one in seven days, breaking the record in New Orleans for speed in getting to the first position. Then I made Field Coordinator, the next rung on the ladder, within a few months. There were pats on the back, congratulations from those on my up-line—it was intoxicating.

I figured my fortune was made. I was crunching the numbers and concluding I'd be a millionaire by the age of twenty-two. I was the "Wonder Boy," as they called me, attending motivational conferences to share my success story. I met all the greats back then—Tony Robbins, Les Brown, and Zig Ziglar. Basketball was old news; I was the next tycoon, with one hundred fifty people in my downline.

This quick success brought me to the attention of a similar business: LocalNet. I saw immediately it was ACN on steroids. This was 1997, the Internet was still fairly new, and people were dialing up on slow modems. Browsing was all about text and still images, but people could guess what the future held for cyberspace. LocalNet promised it had purchased the technology to quickly transport high-quality video across regular copper lines. It had to be legit, because the son of a celebrated media tycoon was fronting this operation.

My upline business partners and I were invited to Atlanta to witness the technology first hand.

"Think about this," the pitchman said. "Video conferencing is on its way—business meetings between New York executives and their LA clients in real time, face-to-face, over the Net. Or what about millions of people watching first-run movies at home—online? Can you imagine the demand when these things are offered? Well, *we're* going to offer them. We've acquired the tech!"

The punch line was, "Think about getting in on the ground floor of something like that. How vast will your downline be? Think of the residual income!"

He was describing Skype and Netflix before they emerged. We got all the information in Atlanta at a convention center, where roughly two thousand of us salivated over a once-in-a-lifetime opportunity to seize the coming market by the jugular.

The requirement was to walk away from our current business. Dad was not as willing as I was to start over, but he agreed. We poured everything into LocalNet. The lure of massive wealth is incredibly seductive. I was dropping in on Ferrari salesrooms, sizing up my next ride. Maybe I'd buy a Ferrari *and* a Lamborghini. At twenty-one, I was a master of the universe—at least my own.

Sure enough, for a year and a half, the business grew like wildfire on the incredible picture we painted for customers, a picture of an Internet video era that was yet to arrive. It was like a fresh lemonade stand in the Sahara. Who wouldn't put their money down? The actual capability hadn't caught up to the sales pitch yet, but that made it all the more enticing. It was always *just about* to hit the market—don't delay, act today! The longer it took for the steak, the more sizzle we had to sell.

More than a thousand people were in my downline—some as customers, many building their own businesses. One of them was Pastor Celoria, the father of some friends of mine at Carey, who was interested in helping his church earn passive income to eliminate debt.

I told him, "Imagine what you can do for your church—and *with* your church—through an opportunity like this, Pastor. It's perfect for someone like you."

"I don't know," he said. "It sounds like quite an opportunity, something that might really help us out. But you have to understand—I'm speaking for all our people, my whole congregation. They trust me. If I put up their money, this *must* work. I can't go back to them and tell them their money's gone with nothing to show for it. I need your word that you and your company are trustworthy."

"Absolutely, Pastor Celoria," I smiled, without hesitating. "You have my word. All our people are gaining wealth already. You'll never regret it. Having this kind of financial freedom will change your life and the lives of everyone in your church."

Pastor Celoria shook my hand, and he bought into the organization with his church—500 customers and consultants in his downline, in no time. It was a huge boost to my business.

By 1998 I had graduated from Carey and was working the business full-time. I was building wealth every day. That's when a call came in from LocalNet's central office. "Listen, head's up: we're no longer in business," said the service rep on the other end.

"What are you talking about? We can't be 'no longer in business'! We're selling the product right and left."

"Well, we've run into some legal issues. You need to advise your downline they won't be getting paid from here on out."

How could that be? We all frantically called each other and compared notes. It turned out that LocalNet was a pyramid scheme, there was no video technology to fill our promises, and the company had gone under. Lawsuits abounded. And not only were we not going to be paid for our sales—the people beneath us weren't going to be paid, either. All those promises, all that "in on the ground floor" adrenalin, had drained away in an instant.

We found out later that when the tech was originally demonstrated in Atlanta, video was impressively transmitted from one computer to another—except that there was no modem involved. The first computer was simply linked to the second one through a cable. Apparently it was a desperate "fake it 'til we make it" ploy, except they didn't ever make it.

We were one of a thousand such stories. This was late in 1998, the front end of the famous "dot-com bubble" that happened over the next year, when all the frantic Internet investments imploded and threw the country into a recession.

So there I was. Phone calls to my downline, with explanations and apologies, were difficult to make, but I could handle them, one by one.

All except the call to Pastor Celoria.

I couldn't face this man of God. I had looked into his eyes and asked for his trust, and he had given it to me. I wasn't responsible for the company's failure, but I was the face of the company to him. In an act of cowardice, I got rid of my cell phone, changed my number, covered my tracks, and moved on. Or made the attempt.

I discovered the impact of moral guilt. Now I carried a little weight on my heart wherever I went. I would think of Pastor Celoria often, wondering about the impact of the loss on his congregation. How would he have expressed his anger to me? It chilled me in the depths of my conscience.

A few days earlier, I'd had the world by both hands. I was on my way to becoming extravagantly wealthy and influential. Just like that, I was out of work and out of money and not even vaguely interested in another traditional business venture, especially with the American economy tanking.

I went into a state of depression, although I didn't know it at the time. What I also didn't know was that I would cross Pastor Celoria's path again one day, with consequences that would have been impossible for me to imagine.

God plants a few surprises along our trails. He was already at work in a number of ways, but I couldn't have seen it even if I'd had any semblance of spiritual wisdom.

For me, it felt like walking off the basketball court in anger. Or out of the honors program at Holy Cross. Or flailing at a weak attempt to "be Christian."

Another role that had shined, only to flame out in the end.

Chapter 5

A MAN WALKS INTO A BAR . . .

H as this ever happened to you? Suddenly you're twenty-something, school is behind you—and you have no idea what happens next.

Up to now, the road was well-marked. But now you're supposed to arrive at your destination: adulthood. An enjoyable career. Family and everything that entails. But here you are, standing at a crossroad that splinters off into a thousand paths.

Your friends move on with life. Some get married, others move away. Buddies are too busy to hang out, trying to build a career. You're back at home.

Robert Frost once said that home is the place where, when you go there, they have to take you in. Mom and Dad are more than happy to see you; you'll always have a home under their roof. Still, they're kind of wondering what's next for you.

Mom and Dad knew quite well I already had some business experience, including an epic business catastrophe on my résumé. I'd built a huge downline that was definitely down on me. I was burned out on that rat race. I told myself, "I have no business doing business."

For lack of anything better to do, I got involved in Brazilian jiujitsu (BJJ) at a gym in Metairie, Louisiana. If it was true I had no money and no clue where I was heading, I did carry a two hundred eighty-five-pound body, one filled with nervous energy, restlessness, and frustration. The gym was a good place to work all that stuff out of my system.

Let me put it this way—I was wrestling with my future and decided my future was wrestling. At least for the time being.

Pulling people down to the mat and grappling with them was surprisingly satisfying. BJJ is designed to help the smaller guy leverage his resources to hold up against a larger attacker. In most of our matches, of course, I was the larger attacker, but I enjoyed the precision and skill of martial arts, and, as with every other talent, I went after it with passion and a determination to excel.

My teacher had trained with the Gracie family. Carlos and Hélio Gracie, the founders of BJJ, adapted the techniques of judo, developed them into something new, and trained their family and followers, such as my teacher. It was all about taking the fight down to ground level, which in some ways felt like the story of my life. I was grappling with something, that's for sure.

I aspired to be in the UFC, the Ultimate Fighting Championship of mixed martial arts. In those days, the late nineties, the UFC was only five years old and a far smaller operation than it is today. There were "War of the Worlds" international competitions where you might see a Brazilian jiujitsu master take on someone from the world of kickboxing or karate, along with mixed techniques from other fighting disciplines. In time, its popularity exploded and led to big TV contracts, but when I was involved, none of us had health insurance. Your fight payout wasn't enough to pay your medical bills after the fight. I never fought profession-ally, only matches in the dojo with guys my size training for fights.

So one Saturday night I was at Tony Angelo's with my parents, trying to figure out what came next for me. The answer was Gene.

He was a man who walked into the restaurant, sized me up, and introduced himself. Gene said, "You're a big guy, and I'm guessing you know how to handle yourself. I don't know what you do for a living, but I have an idea that might be worthwhile for both of us."

I said, "Tell me more."

"Robby, you ever been uptown during Mardi Gras?"

I laughed. "Always."

"Well, if you don't have a problem throwing guys out of a bar for causing problems, then you may be the man I'm look-ing for. I need a head bouncer for my nightclub."

He described the job, the hours, and the pay, and all I could say was, "A job where I'm paid to fight? I'm in."

My life at the time was all about two things: hanging around bars and fighting. Now a guy walks up and says he wants to pay me for doing what I'm already doing. This was the start of the wildest season of my life, which is saying something.

Gene didn't want me to be a bouncer; he wanted me to hire a few other guys to build an army of head-crackers. I went back to the dojo where I trained and asked my big-gest, craziest buddies whether they wanted to make enough money to pay their doctor bills and actually have a little extra—guys like Duane, who was bald with a full goatee and a striking resemblance to Stone Cold Steve Austin.

Lots of nights could be crazy, but one particular night things were five steps beyond crazy. Maybe it was a full moon. I don't remember that, but I do know we needed reinforcements.

One brawl was going on in the bar, and another in the parking lot. My earphone was going crazy. I was told to come to the bar, where these two guys were bothering a couple of young women and wouldn't stop. I brought Duane with me to ask the guys to leave. They refused, so we grabbed them and pushed them along to the door.

But these troublemakers wouldn't give up. Now they were pounding on the outside of the door, shouting, still making a scene. We realized they weren't leaving on their own accord. They needed an escort to the parking lot to get them off our premises.

We hauled them out to the lot, with them kicking and screaming and cursing at us. After they were dumped at their car and warned one last time to leave and not come back, one of them suddenly pulled a nine-millimeter pistol from under the driver's seat. "*Now* tell me what to do! Go ahead, say it one more time!"

The guy was drunk, raging, and I realized with great clarity that my whole life, my whole story could end right here, in a puddle of blood and stupidity.

I saw the gun before Duane did, and I pulled him back. Time screeched to a halt for a moment, a standoff—and then all four of us heard the beautiful music of a police siren.

The police had been called, and they arrived with impeccable timing. The two trouble-makers ditched the gun and took off on foot with the police in hot pursuit. Duane and I just looked at each other and resumed breathing.

The two guys were actually caught, and all's well that ends well.

Sort of.

I kept thinking back to the shimmer of that pistol in the starlight, and thought, *What if?* This was a wake-up call. I lucked out this time, but this moment could come around again. I had no desire to die in a bar parking lot.

I was rooming with Gene, my boss, by this time, and I told him I was a little spooked by the whole incident. I wanted to stay in the bar business, but maybe tone down the rough stuff a few notches. Gene knew me pretty well by this time. He understood I had people skills as well as toughness, and he said, "How'd you like to tend bar?"

"Seriously? You'd let me do that?"

"Why not? You learn to mix the drinks, be friendly with the clientele, keep things lively so they keep ordering— you'd be good at it."

In the nineties, everybody wanted to be like Tom Cruise's character in *Cocktail*, the rock star of the bar with worshipful customers all around him. I'd been paid to fight for a while; now I was going to be a paid class clown, and still in a place I associated with good times. Not bad.

We had a setup like the one in the *Cheers* TV show, with a central bar, a dance area to the side, and a back bar area. But naturally, I was given the back bar, where nobody went. They passed by on their way to the bathrooms. It was pretty dull, actually, not to mention how poor the tips were. After a couple of weeks I began to beg for my shot at the main bar. "You know I can handle it," I said.

I'd actually gotten a little bit of experience as a radio DJ during college. A buddy of mine had a show, and he let me sit in and learn how he selected songs, spliced and edited bits of audio tape together, connected with the listeners, and that kind of thing. One night when a guy called in sick, I even got to be the main guy. I loved it. Now, as a would-be star bartender, I had an idea for a kind of bar-DJ mash-up, where I could be a little more of an entertainer, setting myself apart.

I had a friend named Matt, and we had great chemistry in doing comedy. Gene took it under consideration and finally said, "Matt, I'm going to let you have your own night of the week to do anything you want—you two guys. Test the boundaries. See what works and doesn't work. Go ahead and have some fun."

"Great! I'm ready now—which night am I on?"

"Sunday."

"Sunday? Is the bar even open on Sundays?"

He knew that nobody goes to a bar on Sunday night— well, except maybe the really hard-core drinkers, and that wasn't the crowd I was going after. I needed the party atmosphere that comes with a weekend, or almost any night other than Sunday. But he was willing to open on a normally dead evening and see what we could do.

On our first Sunday night, Matt and I did our thing, then split a buck-twenty-five in tips at closing time. It was that grim; nobody showed up. A week later, it was pretty much the same scene—a few really somber drinkers, and our act was going nowhere.

On the third Sunday, in a moment of inspiration, we saw a few guys over at the pool table. I grabbed the mic and began to announce the shots as if we were on ESPN.

"Ladies and gentlemen, boys and girls, children of all ages, welcome to the Green and Red Eight-Ball Championship Match. I'm your host, Robby Gallaty. With me is Matt Jones."

Matt jumped right in with me. "Guy with the cap is chalking up, has his eyes on that three! Do you think—"

"No way! No way, Matt. Three's a sucker shot. He's gotta cut that five into the side first!"

"He's doing it! I can't believe this! He's aiming at the three! No pressure at all, guy with the cap!"

"Pandemonium, Matt. Sheer pandemonium. The place is going crazy!"

"Cue ball careens off—it's going . . . going . . ."

"SCRATCH! CAP GUY SCRATCHES! IT'S OVER!"

There was no crowd going crazy, of course, except the three guys over by the pool table. They were doubled over, unable to shoot from laughing. At the bar and the tables, people were starting to look up, look at each other, chuckle . . .

This was something nobody had seen at a bar. The next week some of them were back to see if it happened again, and a few of them brought friends. Word-of-mouth began to build interest. We did sportscasts of all kinds of stuff, then we'd take breaks and chat with the people at the bar.

"I think we ought to take this to another level," I mentioned to Matt as we closed up the bar.

"You think anyone will come for that?"

"There's only one way to find out."

Matt and I decided to give it a whirl. We needed to do a whole program. I went out and bought a bunch of video equipment, and now we could actually bring in the comedy instead of fabricate it. Our potential was as wide as our imagination.

I was like that amplifier in *Spinal Tap* with the dial that goes to eleven instead of just ten. I do everything full blast—and we fully had a blast. Our model was Tom Green, who was a new hit on MTV in those days with his form of "guerilla humor," going out and making funny things happen, sharing it with his audience.

We went all over New Orleans and into the bayou, filming—imitating intrepid crocodile hunters stalking an obviously fake, inflatable croc and rubber snakes falling from the tree branches. We'd walk through the French Quarter, asking crazy questions—the kind of thing now common-place on late night TV, but very new and fresh at the time. All of it would go up on the screen at the bar, and people would stop to watch, laugh, applaud, and leave generous tips.

Larger crowds were coming now, which was an amazing thing for a bar on a Sunday night. Once again, my whole identity was wrapped up in the role I was playing. I was surf-ing on the adrenaline of laughter and acclaim, loving every minute, and Matt had to leave—wait, what?

"What do you *mean* you have to leave, Matt?"

"It's August. School is starting up, and I have to go back. You knew that."

"But what about—what about our show?"

"Oh, you'll come up with a new guy."

As if! The act was based on this chemistry that we'd cultivated over months. Too bad, Matt was gone, and I had to regroup.

I talked to my friend Chris from high school, and he sug-gested we rebuild the show all around me, with more of a sidekick than a full partner. And he had a real brainstorm. "You sell cars with your dad, right? That's the world you know, so build your comedy around that experience. We'll call it 'The Closer's Corner,' and your thing is, you're always trying to sell something. That kind of comedy writes itself. So the first thing is, you go infomercial-style."

I said, "I like the way you think." Everybody saw late night infomercials, and it was a medium that cried out for parody.

"The second thing is, you're going to go on location, just like you did with Matt. People love seeing you in recogniz-able local spots. Maybe in these segments you're trying to buy something instead of sell it. You might even work in a magic trick in the least expected place."

"Okay—yeah," I said, the wheels turning in my head already.

"And third, we'll do something with you going back and forth with your cohost."

"Who's my cohost?"

"I have an idea about that."

He explained his idea, and I said, "Hey, I know a guy."

There was a guy we knew from middle school named Randy. We found him sitting on the sofa smoking and drinking. Perfect. "How'd you like to be a star?" I asked.

"Okay," he said calmly, taking another swig. "Except I don't like talking or nothing."

"That's the best part of the whole thing," I said. "You don't have to."

"I'm in," he said, and belched.

We dressed up Randy in gold Elvis glasses with the cheapest leisure suit we could dig up, and bought him a six-pack of Schlitz beer. He'd come out to the song, "Lit Up" by Buckcherry, climb a ladder, crack a beer, and down it before taking a seat on his couch where he'd do his thing, which was to quietly smoke and drink the entire time. No dialogue at all, though I'd play off him and work him into the conversation.

The audiences loved every minute of it. I wouldn't consider it appropriate now, and we'd find it politically incorrect to be sure. Alcoholism is no joke. But this is where I was, and certainly where downtown New Orleans was, in the late nineties.

My theme song was "Eye of the Tiger." Music blaring, I'd walk out in a full suit with blue-shaded, silver-rimmed glasses. There was nothing else like our act on the bar scene.

Soon we were selling T-shirts and videos, bringing in extra money, and packing the place out. People regularly stood outside the bar just to catch a glimpse. Then Gene added a cover charge. That sounded like good news to me. "I'm not making any money at the bar," I told Gene, "because obviously I can't work that while I'm performing. So what's my cut of the door proceeds?"

He looked at me as if I were crazy. "You're joking, right? Answer is zero. I just hired you as a bartender."

"After the way I've built this audience? And on Sunday nights, when you had almost no business? That's not fair at all, Gene!"

He shrugged. The way he saw it, he was the owner and everyone else worked by the hour and for whatever tips they could manage.

"Well, if that's how it works," I said, "then I'm nothing special. You could just hire another bartender to write and perform a show. Because, if you don't give me a cut of the door, I'm gone before next Sunday night."

I guess you've got to know when to hold 'em, and know when to fold 'em. He said "Okay" and wished me luck.

Gene called my bluff, and that was the end of my rock-star-of-the-bar career. I'd burned through another identity and was right back at square one.

Before I closed down that act, however, there had been a particularly big show. It was Labor Day weekend, and the place was packed. On a holiday weekend, the city was always rocking. Knowing it would be a great night, I'd invited my family to come and see what I did. I knew they'd be proud of their son who was making all these people laugh.

What I hadn't thought at all about was that the main skit required me to wear cheap spandex tights in an attempt to sell a workout video. The outfit was highly unflattering in the worst way, and I looked out and saw the sadness in my mother's eyes. It was embarrassing, and it wasn't the reaction I'd been going for.

In that moment, in a flash of insight, I saw myself as my family saw me—a clown who would do pretty much anything in the world for a laugh. What kind of acceptance was I going for? Didn't my parents give it to me?

Of course they did. They loved me lavishly, unconditionally, perfectly. In their eyes, I could do no wrong. I didn't need to be anything other than who I was. Yet I stood now in my skintight spandex, debasing myself for the applause of inebriated strangers.

For one instant, the look in my mother's eyes caused me to step outside of myself for a touch of true perception. A clue. A wake-up call.

Then the moment evaporated. The show must go on. I delivered my next line, waited for the laughter, and continued the performance.

Chapter 6

AN ABSOLUTE WRECK

Why do things come crashing down, just when you're beginning to fly high?

That was the question I was trying to work out as I drove home from work on November 22, 1999. I'd been knocking on the door of financial success, and it all blew up in my face. So I'd switched doors. I'd knocked on the door of fame and acclaim—same thing.

Was it me? No way! Was I jinxed? Who knew?

I was beyond frustrated, but there was nothing I could do but pick myself up, clean myself off, and see what came next.

I was selling cars for Royal Honda in Metairie—a regular paycheck, and that was about it. I could connect with people and move vehicles, and I knew my way around cars and all their features from working with Dad. So I had the pleasure of being pretty good at sales.

Yet I felt deep inside I was meant for greater things than hitting monthly quotas on a car lot. I felt I had gifts. I was two for two in proving myself—in business ability and then in creative entertainment. For me, life felt like a game of Monopoly, where I was just about to land on Boardwalk, but

I kept drawing the card that sends you back to "Go" without collecting $200.

So, back to square one.

———

It was late on a Monday, three days before Thanksgiving, and I was on my way home from the Honda dealership in Metairie, heading east toward Chalmette, cigarette in hand, lost in my thoughts. I never saw the eighteen-wheeler that slammed into me.

He was merging from I-10, and I was coming in from 610. I was in his blind spot as our vehicles approached the same location. His truck slammed into my left rear bumper, which locked our two vehicles together. The semi shoved me into the right guardrail.

My bumper ripped off, and the truck slowed for an instant, then kept moving. To my great fortune, another driver saw the whole thing, and he wouldn't let the truck flee the scene. He chased him down, and the truck driver had no choice but to pull over.

My Mustang was one of Dad's fix-up jobs. He's terrific at rebuilding totaled vehicles, but on this one, there had been a hairline fracture to the seat frame in the earlier collision. You'd never have known it except that now, with a truck slamming into it, the frame didn't have enough strength to hold up. As a result, my seat broke off the hinges as my seat belt locked, and I was hurled to the right side of the interior.

As the car came to a stop, I was thinking what everybody does in that situation: "I could have died just now." Given the speed and mass of the eighteen-wheeler, this could have been fatal to me, and I understood that. What I couldn't have known was that it would set events into motion in my life that were almost fatal in another way.

For now, I was shaken up and hurting all over. I hobbled out of my car and checked out the damage to my Mustang. Pretty bad. The truck driver, defensive and ready to intimidate, was walking back in my direction. "This was your fault!" he said. "You came over into my lane."

"I don't think so! You came out of your lane and slammed me into the rail."

We argued, but to my relief, a witness to the accident soon accompanied the police officer that drove up. The officer wrote the truck driver a ticket, establishing that the law was on my side.

I tried to flex my back as the officer wrote up his account. Looking up ahead to the left, a steeple caught my eye, gleaming over the trees of the neighborhood. It made no impression on me, but it was the perfect symbol of what the future held. What was beneath that particular steeple made all the difference. Behind me lay a traffic accident that would almost doom me; ahead lay a hope that would redeem me.

Death, life, and eternal destiny, together in one place. This was an intersection of more than highways.

I called Dad and told him what had happened. "A truck just hit me from behind on the way home, Dad," I said. "Mustang's in pretty bad shape. Totaled again, I'd say."

"Never mind the Mustang, son, are *you* okay?"

"I'll be all right. A little sore."

More than a little sore as the evening drew on. All I could do was take a few ibuprofen, but the next day my doctor took a good look at me. He checked out the X-rays and told me I had two herniated disks in the neck and two in the back. "You were messed up pretty good," he stated. "You might need surgery down the road. And I imagine you're in some pain."

The doctor went out of the room and came back with a prescription for Vicodin and muscle relaxers. Vicodin combines an opioid (hydrocodone) with acetaminophen. I filled the script and used them as directed, every four to six hours, which took the edge off the pain.

For the next two months, I lived my life and endured my job with the help of the pain pills. I knew I'd heal, though I couldn't train to fight anymore. Most of my attention went to getting paid by the trucking company to repair my car. I had no thought of any injury-related lawsuit; all I wanted was eight thousand dollars to cover repairs—eight thousand dollars the trucking company eventually told me I was never going to get, unless I took them to court.

Ridiculous—now I had to find a lawyer just for the car repairs in an accident that wasn't my fault. I'd never worked with a lawyer before—didn't even know one. But I did know a guy from my network marketing experience. He had a friend who had gotten a large settlement with a personal injury attorney. I made the connections, and the lawyer took it from there.

When we met, the attorney wanted to know all about my condition, what the doctor had said, and what kind of pain I was in. I told him about my Vicodin and muscle relaxers, and he nodded quickly and said, "I've got a doctor who can give you a little more help than that."

I had no experience in this world of serious pain narcotics. I'd never heard anything about an opioid crisis, and I didn't know how addiction worked. None of that ever crossed my mind, and nobody warned me.

I wish they had.

This new doctor, who clearly had a referral relationship with the attorney, sent me home with a whole arsenal of addictive pain drugs: Oxycontins, Somas, Percocets, and Valiums. All of these could be dangerous—especially mixed together.

I quickly discovered these pills worked just like magic. I might be lying in bed, unable to sleep because of the pain. Or I might be invited to go clubbing with friends, but I'd be aching. As long as I had my pills, everything was good. My choice was between pain that kept me from living a normal life and a high that felt better than normal life. At first, it's about pain; later, it's about the high. I began by taking pills only when necessary; then, I actually looked for excuses to take the pills more and more.

But it was all very discreet. I could get through a work-day, sell a couple of Hondas, visit my parents, and go to a bar. My life seemed absolutely normal to everyone else, all while using my meds. As a matter of fact, I had Herculean energy.

I'd climb into my car and store my pain meds right there in the center console of my car without thinking twice—that's how new at this stuff I was.

I told a buddy about this, and his eyes got wide as he heard about where I kept my stuff. "Dude," he said. "Never, ever leave your drugs in the car! That's like leaving money in plain sight on the dashboard. Same thing."

"Really? Who would steal somebody's pain pills?"

"Robby. Are you clueless? Do you know how much those things sell for on the street? Five bucks a pop for a Percocet. Twenty bucks for Oxys."

"People sell these on the street?"

"Every day. It would take you less than five minutes to walk downtown and buy some."

I'd never heard of anything like that. I assumed drug dealers trafficked in cocaine or Meth, not the little pills your druggist gave you at the pharmacy. I looked at my pain meds and saw them in a whole new light. These thoughts rolled around in my brain and attached themselves to my interest in network marketing. What if . . .

Suddenly I had a new idea for making a little extra money. As long as I could get prescriptions for the drugs, I could sell what I had and generate enough income to cover replacements—plus extra cash, of course.

I was capable of thinking like that in those days, though I rationalized it to some extent. I saw myself as distributing "harmless" muscle relaxants and pain relievers—not heroin or crystal meth. It was just a little casual profit-making among friends. At least that's what I told myself, and that's how it began.

I asked my buddy a few more questions, and he confirmed that he had friends who knew where to buy and sell these pills. "Can you introduce me to them?" I asked him. "I have an idea for us to make serious money."

I'd been able to sell phone service, and even video technology that was not yet released to the public; how much more successful could I be with pills that could be popped right there on the spot? I knew I could move them like candy.

My friend started introducing me to others, and I explained how we could set up a network, create our own downlines—all the basics. At the same time, I tapped into old friends from the past who dealt drugs under the radar— all the while we had been friends, and I had no clue.

As for business-building, some of them looked at me like I was crazy. "I just like getting high, man," they said. "What you're talking about sounds like work!" I eventually connected with two guys: Rick, who would be my roommate, and Rodney. Both had aspirations of making money to support our lifestyle.

I pushed on with the idea. I could still go to the second doctor, and he had no problem sending me home with fresh supplies of narcotics. But if I ran out, it was a lot easier to find a friend on the street and buy from him than to wait for an upcoming doctor's appointment.

There were guys who looked at the pills just the way they thought of alcohol—they came to it to get high. But there were many others like me—people who had started off with a genuine need to relieve the pain but had gotten hooked. Eventually they found themselves on the street feeding their addiction. Wherever the starting point, we all ended up in the same place—buying and using in parking lots and dark corners of bars.

That's how a national health crisis begins.

———

As I checked in with my attorney, eager to find out about getting paid for the repairs to my car, I found he was very interested in my pain and my use of prescription narcotics. "Car payment?" he asked. "They owe you much more than that, son! Look at what they've done to you. They've made you dependent on pain medication. The truck hit you, and his company refused to do anything about it. They've ruined your life, and they owe you hundreds of thousands of dollars at least!"

I thought about the way he had pushed me toward a doctor he worked with, one who was eager to get me taking more of the drugs. The second doctor had vastly improved the odds I'd become addicted by sending me home with four kinds of drugs. I had to wonder what kind of back deal the doctor had with my attorney, who now had a more substantial case. And the thought of it made me sick. That just made me want another Valium.

I was still one of the regulars in various bars and nightclubs, and of course my new crowd hung out in those places, too. I was pursuing club DJing at this point. I'd purchased a set of Numark turntables—standard equipment for that field. I'd have said that was my new high, except I already had a new high. The two went well together. You needed energy for hours if you wanted to be the life of the party in these places.

After a couple of months of taking the pills, one of my friends said, "Robby, it's time for you to take the next step."

"What next step?"

"It's called Ecstasy," he grinned.

"I'm not so sure I want to get into serious stuff like that."

"You don't know what you're missing. I ain't kidding, man—it'll change your life forever. First one's my treat." Those pills went for about twenty-five bucks apiece. I knew that Ecstasy was always in high demand.

"Maybe another night," I said. My friend stayed on me, though. He kept telling me I had to try this amazing experience. After I couldn't put him off any longer, on a Thursday night, and in a weak moment, I told him I'd try a tab. "You won't be sorry. Tell you what, I'll split one with you," he said. "You'll get a taste."

I examined the bland, rose-colored half-pill, so small and innocent looking, and placed it on my tongue.

As soon as I swallowed it, my friend let out a whoop of joy. "No turning back now. You better strap yourself in for the ride."

We sat around my place for a while until it started to kick in. I noticed the effects within fifteen minutes. I was talking more than usual. I felt very open, eager to be transparent. I could talk about anything. We had music playing in the apartment, and it sounded wonderful, incredible. It moved me. I had never felt quite like this before.

"How's it going, Robby?"

"You weren't lying," I said.

"I told you!" He looked at his watch. "Escapades is opening."

This was a club in Metairie that was only open from 10:00 p.m. to 6:00 a.m. I walked through the doors for the first time. The bass from the subwoofers took my breath away as we entered. I immediately noticed yellow glow sticks in the hands of other partyers lining the dance floor. We danced, drank, and stayed until the place was shutting down. Everything at Escapades, every friend, every conversation was amplified. In two hours, I had to be at work—and that felt like it could be fun, too.

That night was the beginning of an all-out dependency on drugs and the life that came with it. The more I used, the more cash I needed to buy. So I expanded my operation. I sold not only pills but an expensive and effective form of marijuana through a connection I had from my network marketing days. I met my clients through selling cars.

I'd carry my zip-locked package in the trunk, make some deliveries at lunchtime, finish my workday, and at night, I was training to be a stockbroker. I left the car business to pursue another career during this period, my parents wanting to steer me in the right direction. I also sold GHB, a liquid high, through another connection I had. There was something for everybody, a drug for every situation. Maybe if my mind had been straight more often, if I hadn't been either high or thinking about a high, I'd have realized I was on a road that led deep into the wilderness, and if I went far enough, there would be no turning back.

Perhaps my saving grace was that I didn't like blood and needles. That's the fastest road to death for a lot of addicts, and I had my second-grade self to thank for my refusal to inject anything. At the age of seven, I came down with walking pneumonia and almost died. My teacher was good enough to come to the hospital and teach me on her own time, so that I wouldn't fail second grade (once again, my parents behind the scene, working everything out to give me the best life possible). But the whole hospital experience left me with a dread of needles. As an addict, I had many friends who shot something into their veins, and I noticed those were the ones most likely to be goners.

Spoiler alert: God was looking out for me. Like my parents, he was behind the scene, working out the foolish and sinful decisions I was making in a way that would turn out for my good. I couldn't see it yet, but I would one day.

NB·

For a while, I felt on top of the world. Immortal. Unstoppable. Ecstasy has its name for a reason. But artificial ecstasies never last. Eventually, I'd come down and face another work day that was less and less interesting to me. When I wasn't high, nothing in the world was interesting other than the idea of the next high.

Somebody said that sin takes you farther than you want to go, keeps you longer than you want to stay, and costs you more than you want to pay. Drugs are the perfect expression of that. Who doesn't want to feel great? Who checks the map to see where the trail eventually leads? Nobody ever starts out thinking, "I have a long-term plan to destroy my life."

We should come into this world with a warning label: Don't fall for your false sense of control. "I can do this, and I can pull back when I need to." Addicts believe they can quit whenever they want, until they actually try to do it.

Eventually I realized I was trapped. I wanted to get out of the trap, but I didn't know how. My life wasn't what I'd planned. The former lead guitarist of a Christian band shouldn't be selling pills in dark nightclubs. My friends weren't a very admirable crowd, and I had deep secrets I had to keep from my family at all costs.

Like the car that started the whole thing, my life was an absolute wreck.

Chapter 7

DOWNHILL RACING

C. S. Lewis once wrote that the surest road to hell is the gradual one, with a gentle slope you almost fail to notice—no sharp turns or signposts. It winds downward to its destination without your even noticing it.[1]

I know that road well. It's just that I've never been a slow driver; when I head somewhere, I head there at full speed.

My descent into full-scale drug abuse was amazingly rapid. In November of 1999, before the accident, I was selling cars, training for the UFC, and thinking about business opportunities. By early the next year, I was looking for faster and better drug connections. I got in too deep for a number of reasons, all having to do with my wiring.

Addictive personalities are the ones at highest risk to be devastated by alcohol, drugs, sex, or almost anything else. I don't possess every mark of the typical addictive personality, but I do have some key traits.

First, I was born with ADHD, so *any* kind of stimulation, any shiny thing dangled before me, was all but irresistible. ADHD people chase the dopamine surge nonstop.

Needless to say, life is full of highs and lows alike, but a *chemical* high is in a class by itself. There's a parable in the Bible about a "pearl of great price." A man searches everywhere for fine pearls, but when he finds the one that outshines them all, he'll sell everything he has to possess it. My pearl, at this point, was the ultimate high; the day would come when I would find something greater than any riches found on earth; the true "precious pearl" that doesn't enslave. In 2000, I only knew the thrills of the physical world.

Second, I was a fully functioning addict. Not everyone can live that way, but I did. It enabled me to lead a shadow life by compartmentalizing my drug abuse so that the people who loved me most knew nothing about it. It meant I could cut off my parents and my sister from getting me help. Other than God himself, the greatest resource available to us, in times of crisis, is the love of the people who care about us. But true love always demands full transparency—my family needed to know what was going on in order to help, but I covered it up so well, they had no idea.

During this period, I never hid away from my family. We had dinner, we went to the movies, we hung out together— but all the time my parents had no clue their son was a drug abuser and dealer. I also went to work every day, I did my job, and everything seemed normal.

But I was secretly continuing to destroy myself.

Third, and with tragic irony, I was a born networker, entrepreneurial to the core. I loved interacting with people and stepping up to lead them, empowering them to accomplish a greater purpose. Like every other skill I had, this one was made for greater things. I was just misusing my gifts.

Practically my first impulse on being introduced to drug use was to start building distribution networks. That meant I was good at making money on narcotics, which only meant more narcotics were at my disposal. I was simply too proficient and creative at feeding the beast.

A guy named Rocky worked for my dad. One day I was hanging out at the collision center, and we got into a conversation. We were close enough that I'd let him in on my secret. He'd told me in the past that he was prone to taking too many Somas, so he would "walk around in the Soma coma like a zombie." He was a great body man for car repair, but of course my dad knew nothing about what he did in his spare time.

"My only problem," I said, "is that I can't get my meds fast enough. My new doctor writes pretty good prescriptions, but it's still not as many as I can move or use. I could really make some money if I had a better source."

"You need two doctors," said Rocky.

"So how am I supposed to do that? Don't they stop you from doing that stuff?"

"Not if they don't know. You'll have to fill the scripts at different pharmacies not to be detected. Also, always pay cash. I know a doctor who will write you up ninety of each prescription. I've done this for years."

"Where do I find him, and how do I get in?"

"It's a *she*. Dr. Casey is her name,[2] and I'll give you directions. She has a pain management clinic over in New Orleans east. It's in kind of a rough area, but you just walk in, pay something like a hundred and fifty bucks, and she'll pull out her pad without asking many questions. You'll just have to wait a while. Remember, make sure you take it to a different drug store."

I drove to the place he told me about on Chef Menteur Highway and walked in. I should have known—the waiting room was packed wall to wall. Most of the people I would have guessed were drug addicts, rather than the kind of uptown, "recreational" user I considered myself to be. Could I be staring at a possible future—the place where the road leveled out, at the very bottom of that road with no signposts?

The thought never crossed my mind. I was in full control. I could stop anytime I wanted, like all the other addicts.

This wasn't your typical medical practice; it was open from late afternoon until very early in the morning. Off-duty cops stood at the door and in the waiting room. It was a crime-ridden area, and prostitutes hung out nearby looking for business. Dr. Casey even kept a pistol with her.

Many of the cars in the lot had license plates from out of state, and payment was cash only—this place was definitely "out of network." They didn't even try to file insurance.

I sat smoking through a pack of cigarettes, waiting for three or four hours and checking my watch impatiently. This gave me time to think of ways to use my business expertise and come up with a way to avoid camping out in the waiting room.

Sure enough, the doctor owned a BMW that was all but totaled. "I think we can help each other," I told her. "We'll have Rocky fix your car at my dad's shop without paying your deductible, and you let us go to the head of the line whenever we visit."

When things couldn't seem to get any "better" for me, I got even luckier. While Rocky was working on her car, he found a blank prescription pad in her trunk. There's nothing more dangerous than a prescription pad that's found its way into the hands of the wrong people.

"This is even better than going to the head of the line," I said. "Can we just write our own prescriptions?"

"We're gonna have to forge the doctor's name," said Rocky.

"That's no problem. I used to forge my dad's signature back in the day on most of my report cards in school. I can trace Casey's writing and learn to imitate it perfectly. Not that anybody takes a second look. We just need to go back to the doc one more time, get her signature on a prescription, and we can go from there."

In the present day, when we have data networks in the cloud, the various pharmacies and doctors keep tabs on people. They know who you are and what you're taking, so this particular scam wouldn't work. But in early 2000, we could get away with it. Double our drugs, double our funds. The typical prescription would cost me four hundred dollars to fill, and sell quickly on the street for fifteen hundred or so—a nice profit margin with no taxes involved.

Given my compulsive nature, of course, I'd often end up snorting the whole thing myself instead of selling any of it. Then there would be a week with empty medicine bottles before I could return to the office for another script.

I remember the moment I realized how close to the edge I was.

That day, I wrote myself a prescription on the pad and took it into a drugstore I'd never visited in the past. It looked safe enough. I walked up to the pharmacist's counter and laid down the slip of paper. The man picked it up, looked up from it with a smile, and said, "Hi, Mr. Gallaty. Did you see the doctor today?"

"Yes, I did." I tried to smile calmly, look him in the eye, and seem casual.

"This will take me about thirty minutes, okay?"

He carried the prescription around the corner, and I heard him pick up a phone. I realized he was going to verify that what he had was genuine. My heart began to beat rapidly. The pad, of course, came from the doctor who ran the pain clinic. I suddenly realized he just might be suspicious of Dr. Casey. A guy the pharmacist doesn't know walks into his drugstore, he's going to be a little more careful about filling a prescription for Oxys and the like. I hadn't given that a thought; I'd just seen the pad and figured it was Willy Wonka's Golden Ticket.

I thought rapidly. Two options came to mind. One, I could jump the counter while the pharmacist was on hold, punch him in the face, and make a quick getaway. But this six-six guy would be IDed quickly and he'd go to jail for assault.

Two, I could roll the dice and see what happened. As I went back and forth, I heard the man say, "Okay, then. I'll call back in a few."

I thought about the pain management clinic and how much of a zoo it was. It was the kind of place where nothing happens quickly or efficiently, and suddenly I was thanking God for that fact. The delay was my grace period.

The pharmacist returned and said, "Your doctor's a little busy, I'll call back in—"

Before he could complete the sentence, I snatched the slip of paper out of his hand and said, "Thanks, I'll just come back later!" And I hustled out the door as the pharmacist watched me in surprise. If he didn't suspect something before, he would now. But I never intended to set foot in that drugstore again.

I called Rocky. "Abort the mission immediately." If it happened to me, it would happen to him—then we'd both be in huge trouble.

Since the introduction of Oxycontin in the nineties, this had become a common crime and the penalties were strict. This was another wake-up call, but I wasn't capable of waking up—not at that moment anyway. I was selling all kinds of drugs, and if I'd stopped selling, I wouldn't be able to buy and use them. It's a vicious cycle. I was known among my crowd as the MVP of the drug world. Friends couldn't believe I'd gone from never trying a drug to full-blown addict in three months; I never went anywhere at half-speed.

———

Not long after that, Spring Break 2000 came around. In the past, I hadn't necessarily been a big spring break guy, but now it had different meaning. College kids go to the beach and a certain number of them buy drugs. If you're a dealer, it's like fishing in a stocked pond, and all you have to do is get there and bait your hook.

On the beach in Panama City are the Moondrifter condos, and right next door is Club La Vela, supposedly the world's largest nightclub. I was one of five guys heading to PCB to do business. Instead of suntan lotion and beach towels, though, we were loaded up with a car full of drugs. But you don't just load these things in suitcases and take off in an SUV—the police, of course, are all over the highways. You take precautions.

We made it there safe and made all the rounds of the spring break beach scene; the only notable thing that happened was that I met a girl and started dating her. This generally doesn't happen at the beach during spring break—people just do some hard-core partying and then go home. But this girl lived in Lafayette, Louisiana, two hours across the state, and we began driving back and forth to see each other.

She shared my interest in getting high and helping others do the same. And once again, she compounded my problem, because she had Mexican drug connections. These people were serious about bringing in drugs from across the border, and our business grew. I was now involved in trafficking hundreds of pills through the network, and I could have done serious time as a federal offender. Somehow that never happened.

As much as I spent my evenings in dance clubs, I gravitated toward the center of attention—the role of DJ. This was my new aspiration; the closest thing to being a rock star in a nightclub is being the one who selects and mixes the music.

There was a real flair to it, a knack for making nightclub magic, keeping the house rocking to its highest potential. Raves—huge dance parties—were at the peak of their popularity during this time. Nonstop, pounding, synthesizer-dominated grooves, played through huge speakers, drew people into these clubs, and a slick DJ knew how to move seamlessly between CD and vinyl.

For me, it was a continuation of what I had done with "Closer's Corner," replacing comedy with music—and to a large extent, liquor with recreational drugs. In 2000 and 2001, I was all about being a techno DJ, just as I'd been all about Brazilian jiujitsu and multilevel networking. It was my new chosen career.

Every club regular knew me, and a lot of them bought from me. My new girlfriend had enlarged my network, and I was able to move uptown to a nice apartment. Most nights we walked into the club at nine or ten, and ended up on Bourbon Street before it was over. We used friends who would distribute whatever drugs we were moving at the time. The evening ended at five or six in the morning, unless we threw a Rave after-party that would last until noon. The party was always at my house, the center of activity for a lot of people caught up in this world.

I remember a lot of crazy things—and I guess it's amazing I can even remember anything at all. One Sunday morning, we decided to be "roof rangers," as we climbed on the roof of our home to read the morning paper. It's a miracle someone didn't plunge to the street below in our stupefied condition. Another time, we climbed into my friend's attic, walked toward the neighbor's attic from there (he lived in a double), dropped down into his home while he was out of town, borrowed his vacuum cleaner, then returned it without being caught.

I never got into trouble—not selling drugs, not getting sketchy prescriptions, not driving to Florida while high. We were bulletproof.

Until we weren't.

One of our closest friends, a big part of our group, died with a heroin needle stuck in his arm. It sent shock waves through us. Maybe he just wasn't careful enough. Maybe we should have picked up on his warning signals. Maybe, maybe—there had to be something different with him. He was dead, but it wasn't going to happen to us.

Until it *did* happen to another one of us. Over a three-year period, I lost eight friends to drugs and alcohol. It was like living in a mystery novel, where characters were being found dead one by one. But the identity of the murderer was no mystery at all. Everyone knew the killer and knew the killer would strike again. But nobody could do anything, because the "killer" was the thing that held us all together and gave our lives meaning.

The killer owned us, and we despised it but continued to serve it as slaves.

We talked about getting out, changing things, moving on with our lives. Detox was a hopeful and completely terrifying word, but if we really thought about it, there were only two potential outcomes: detox or death. The problem was, we didn't really think about it for very long—the drive to the next high was too strong.

Eight dead, six in jail. Those six weren't bulletproof, either. Looking back, there's something very odd about the fact that none of this ever happened to me. Things were happening all around me, after all—things I didn't even know about.

For example, at the New Orleans State Palace Theater, the Drug Enforcement Agency (DEA) began to investigate the raves as a real local crisis, a health epidemic. They knew that, during a two-year period, four hundred teenagers overdosed and ended up in local emergency rooms during fifty-two raves at the State Palace, many of which I attended. The DEA, along with the U.S. Attorney for the Eastern District of Louisiana, began an undercover sting operation called Operation Rave Review in January of 2001. They began arresting dealers, went after the owners and operators of the club, and eventually all but eliminated the drug activity at that particular location.

Soon after their success there, the same investigators moved down to Panama City, to Club La Vela, the place where I met my girlfriend and sold drugs during spring break in 2000. Again, multiple arrests were made. The owners of the club were charged with operating a "crack house."

I also discovered that when I was visiting Dr. Casey, who wrote almost unlimited narcotic prescriptions, there was another visitor sitting in that waiting room—a pharmacist named Dan Schneider. He had carried out a personal investigation of why his son was shot in the head, why it happened during a drug deal, and who had supplied his habit. The web of evidence led to Dr. Casey.

For months, Schneider discreetly watched the crowded office, noticing the strange hours, the out-of-town buyers, and the fact that when Dr. Casey wasn't even present, prescriptions were still being written. He collected compelling evidence.

Eventually, Schneider got federal investigators interested in the case, and eventually the doctor was arrested. They also came down hard on a drug network that originated with her practice, arresting her runners. When SUVs full of federal officers showed up at her house, Dr. Casey smiled cynically and told them they were all dead. She had some dangerous backers.

Somehow I spent this same period of time with all these doomed people. I was in all the wrong places with all the wrong people at all the wrong times. All around me there were deaths and arrests, and some of those people are presumably still doing time. Yet for now, I continued to walk between the raindrops. It was as if the Angel of Death was two steps behind me, but never quite caught up with me.

But the time was rapidly approaching for me to pay my dues. Soon, my sin would find me out, and I would finally come to the end of that long and winding road.

Chapter 8

HITTING BOTTOM

OxyContin made its debut on the pharmaceutical market in 1996. It comes from the same poppy from which we derive opium, which is the key ingredient in heroin. The most active substance in opium is morphine, but OxyContin is 1.5 times more potent than morphine.

When it was first introduced, this wonder drug was a difference-maker in pain management for terminal cancer patients. But its method followed in the tradition of all the opiates: it dispensed euphoria from a handy pill bottle. Or through a patch, a snort, or a shot.

Oxy delivered little doses of the thing every member of the human race desires: a powerful sense of joy and well-being. Or at least something that wore a convincing mask of joy.

It invited you into a world where everything was wonderful, but after a short period of time, the invitation was null and void. The party was over, and just maybe, if you became accustomed to these drugs, you almost began looking forward to the original pain, because it was your return invitation to the party. It was a never-ending journey without a destination. Like a book without a conclusion. We called it "chasing the ghost."

After a while, pain wasn't even a factor. Your drug-induced reality was your life, and the old reality—the *real* reality, where your friends and jobs, issues and sufferings existed—that was no more than the waiting room you had to endure until the door opened again.

OxyContin was the hottest thing in painkillers at century's end, the time when my Mustang was wrecked. In 1998, the previous year, the drug's parent company produced a video called, "I Got My Life Back." Six people with chronic pain were shown living wonderful, blissful lives through OxyContin. A dignified doctor looked into the camera and promised, "No side effects!" These videos were shown in patient waiting rooms of medical practices across America. Everybody wanted a piece of it. Oxy was the new drug store sensation.

In 1999, the year of my accident, opioid prescriptions increased by eleven million. But with that many users, the claim of "no side effects" was quickly debunked. In 2007, executives with Oxy's parent company stood before a judge to plead guilty of misbranding their drug. They settled with the United States government for $635 million.

The problem was, it wasn't the U. S. government with the monkey on its back. Federal lawyers weren't out on the streets searching desperately for a way to feed the habit. I was. My friends were. Hundreds of thousands of us were hooked, and our entire lives were rocked.

In the weeks and months following my wreck, during early 2000, I was the textbook case of opioid addiction. By the grace of God and the love of family, I escaped the death that came to hundreds of thousands of people like me. And though all kinds of controls and regulations have been slapped on the opioid industry, it's still a problem—a crisis, actually. More people died of opioid abuse in 2016 alone than in the entire Vietnam Conflict.

By 2001, when the bottom fell out for me, the crisis was still working up steam. It was clear America had a new drug-related problem, so advisory groups were being created and research was underway. But none of it was in time to help me.

———

I had found that, like every kind of sin, Oxy offered the world but demanded your soul. Drug addiction left absolutely no detail of your life untouched, because you'd do virtually anything for that next high. When could I get my next dose? I'd live in anxiety until I had it, and beyond anxiety, I knew there was the sheer physical hell of withdrawal. I knew on some level what was happening to me, but the next visit to my drug-induced state kept me from having to dwell on that thought.

I lost interest in everything else, which is one reason so much of this period of my life remains a blur, like an impressionistic painting filled with dark, swirling colors but little real detail. It's difficult to reconstruct exactly what happened when. My life existed as a pursuit of a high, and I surrounded myself with fellow pursuers.

Yet my parents and my sister were always there. They weren't quite sure what was up with me—not at first—but they knew something wasn't quite right. I've already mentioned how, in 2000, they set me up in an apartment, bought all the furniture, and arranged for me to train for a career as a stockbroker. They were convinced I'd be a natural. Of course, they believed I could do anything. No matter what I was into, they were my cheerleaders. But if they'd known the truth, they wouldn't have been leading any cheers.

Mom and Dad were excited about my future in the financial world. I had a terrific stock-trading coach whose pupils never failed to pass the Series 7 test. In fact, he was 18 for 18 up to this point. After passing the test, I was promised an office in a high-rise building off Poydras Street in downtown New Orleans as a stockbroker.

During the final section of the exam, I had an attack of nerves and decided to snort some Oxys in the bathroom during the last break. *This should calm me down,* I told myself. It seemed like a great idea at the time. At least nerves made a good excuse to get high. My wrong answers spiraled, and I failed the test by two points.

My parents were throwing me a party to congratulate me. There were refreshments, ice cream, cake, streamers, banners, and friends—and I had to walk in and say, "I'm sorry. It's not happening. I failed." I remember thinking, *How many times do I have to say that?* It was the story of my life.

And of course, for me, that badge of shame was a brand-new excuse to double down on getting high. Everything was an excuse in those days.

———

In 2001, I finally ran out of money. It's an inevitable moment for every abuser—the outgo is always greater than the income, and you can't do much about it.

Users begin taking everything they own to pawn shops, and ultimately there's nothing left to sell but the one thing in your new world: the drug itself. And that's a struggle, because the temptation to use rather than sell your stash is too powerful. So life becomes a vicious cycle that's smaller and tighter every time it comes around—until it resembles a noose.

To keep from strangling, I began stealing from my parents.

As someone who owned his own business, Dad had a credit card he used. He might put thousands of dollars' worth of car parts on it in a single day, so there were pages of charges each month, and I knew he didn't check them too closely. He also entrusted the card, its number, and its expiration date to me during the time I was working for him. I helped him make purchases, ran things while he was out of town, and, most of all, I was his son. He trusted me.

When I began needing money desperately, I realized the power of that credit card number. I could order something over the phone, then turn the brand-new item into cash as soon as it arrived.

I told myself it was a stopgap; I wouldn't do this forever. (I was correct on that count.) All that money was running through the business, and Dad wasn't going to notice. And most important of all, *I needed another high. And I needed it now.*

"Little" sins never stay that way. They grow up. Guilt begins to dissolve like a fine mist, and you become reckless.

I started out using my dad's credit card for my insatiable physical need. But in time, I found it easy to use the card for something I simply wanted: a Fender Stratocaster guitar, along with a pedal and an amp. If there was a tiny whisper in my ear, coming from my conscience, I ignored it. That whisper would have said, "One day, maybe you could say, 'Hey, Dad, it was my body crying out for the drug. I had no choice.' But you can't say that about a guitar. This is simply stone-cold theft, and from the parents who love you."

That's why it was significant it was that guitar—not something I bought and pawned for drugs—that got me caught. It was the most revealing, most shameful example of a pattern of sin that caught me.

I ordered the Fender over the phone, and someone from the company called my dad's office to say, "Mr. Gallaty, your guitar is on back order." My dad's assistant handed him the phone.

"We didn't order any guitar."

The girl on the line confirmed the name on the card. When Dad got off the phone, he called my mom about the mystery—was it identity theft?—and soon they were checking the monthly statement. It wasn't only the guitar they found there, but a number of other strange purchases—nice stuff, expensive stuff. Quickly they pulled out previous bills, and they added up at least $15,000 in bogus charges.

They knew about my interest in guitars, and they also knew I had access to that card number. An "ordinary" identity theft wouldn't have gone on so long—the thief uses information quickly and moves on. Only one person could have stolen from them like this.

I can't imagine how deeply ill, how personally wounded they felt, when the hard truth became clear. *Our son, our pride and joy, is robbing us blind.*

The conversation that followed between my mother and me is terrible to remember—how she told me I was no longer welcome in their home, how hurt my father was. And then the way I snapped back in anger. All of it replayed over and over in my mind like a horror film. We were done, my parents and me.

What followed would be the worst seventy-five days of my life—two and a half months, beginning with a cold February that now seemed far colder. Even while high, I felt the rift between my parents and me, and besides—I was still jobless, out of money, living in an apartment where I couldn't pay the bills. I pushed drugs here and there, but for addicts, money is fleeting. It slips through the fingers like sand.

There was some place in my soul that realized I was completely out of control, this couldn't go on. Something had to give, either my life or my habit. The two couldn't coexist forever.

There weren't many alternatives, really. I could come clean and ask for help. I could move into serious crime. Or, well, maybe I could find some other stopgap and delay the inevitable. For a week, a month, however long.

As far gone as I was, I couldn't fathom "serious" crime— selling pills was one thing, but I wasn't going to get into big-time robbery or cocaine distribution channels.

I wasn't going to come clean, either. Ask for help? I couldn't face the shame of it; there was some tiny element of my pride still holding firm. I hadn't come to the end of myself, which is that one destination we must reach to find any hope.

So I opted for the stopgap. I'd sell even the few possessions I really cared about. My personal things went to the pawnshop; my baseball card and comic book collection; my guitars, amplifiers, and stereo equipment; rings and jewelry. I even tried selling the air-conditioning window unit, but I couldn't figure out who to sell it to. However, pretty soon it was useless anyway, because the power company cut Rick, my roommate at the time, and me off. We had no lights, no water, no gas. All of the furniture my parents picked out for my apartment was gone. I sold everything.

I'd buy drugs with the proceeds, get high, come down, and walk down the same dead end street. Addiction is utterly merciless. The drugs never told you, "Okay, that's enough. You've completely ruined your life. I'll leave you alone now." They just shout even louder, "More! More!"

So I hit absolute bottom.

As the gap in my relationship with Mom and Dad widened, my friendship with Rodney deepened.

Rodney was all in as a dealer. He had an apartment downtown where I often crashed or just hung out. Rodney sold Crystal Meth and Special K (ketamine)—serious drugs he could move quickly on the street. The police knew him as well as I did, and he'd been followed for some time, which is why he moved out of Chalmette.

In Rodney I couldn't help but see my future—someone who no longer thought about turning back. He was in this life for the duration, wherever it led, and he wasn't kidding himself about turning over a new leaf. After the blowup with my parents, I felt like Rodney pointed the way where I was heading. The old world was gone.

My new friend welcomed me with a proposition. "Let's get out of this place," he said. "They know us too well here. Cops will get us sooner or later."

"This is my home," I said. "I love this city. Where would we go?"

"San Diego."

"Why? What's there?"

"A rich life and an easy life. Look—I've done this before. We move to Southern California and rent an apartment. Once a month, we cross the border. It's half an hour to Tijuana, two hours to Ensenada. And Special K comes in 10-mil bottles there, dirt-cheap without a prescription. You load up, fly home, and you're in business."

"Either sell the whole bottle or put the stuff in the oven on a cooking sheet, one or two bottles at a time—heat it up, place it in baggies, and you're done. One trip a month gets you ten or fifteen thousand, and you enjoy your profit the other twenty-five days. No more frantic running around for nickel-and-dime business transactions."

I thought about what he was saying. In Southern California, we'd be safer. And San Diego wasn't a bad place to be. The sun was appealing to someone living in a freezing apartment in February, taking icy cold showers. Seven months later, the window would close forever on anything like this involving airplanes. The attacks on the World Trade Center would see to that. But in February of 2001, you could still pack just about anything on a plane and take it wherever you wanted.

"Come on, dude," said Rodney. "San Diego is sun and surf, a whole new life. Easy money. There's nothing here for you anymore—you have no family, right?"

I looked up at him. The words were like a knife to the heart. It was true, but I didn't like hearing someone else say those words.

"I don't know, Rodney."

He sighed, shook his head, and kept after me for four days. He really needed a buddy to go with him. And he had no choice about leaving. He had a permanent "Go directly to jail" card in New Orleans. He needed a clean slate.

I had every reason to go, nothing tangible to hold me back, and a desperate need for something new. But in the end, I said no. Something deep inside wouldn't let me pull that trigger. I wasn't even sure why, but I chose the current hell over the promise of California.

Call it the "still, small voice" inside. Call it an angel watching out for me, applying some invisible hand of restraint. Whatever it was, I've come to believe there are moments when our lives are teetering on the edge of some abyss, and there's a gentle—or sometimes not so gentle—hand that takes hold of us, shelters us, protects us from our most dangerous threat: our own self-destructive impulses.

That divine hand held me back from California.

Chapter 9

THE PARTY'S OVER

'Ve never spent a colder, more desolate winter.

Rodney left, so I had one friend fewer. As for family, I had nobody but my sister.

Lori would come to see me in that freezing, dark apartment. "Just checking in on you, Robby," she'd say. Then she'd walk past me into the apartment, look around, and say, "How can you live like this?"

I felt ashamed, but at least the gloom of that place might keep her from looking into my eyes.

Lori was in school at the University of South Alabama over in Mobile, working toward an engineering degree. But whenever she was home, she'd faithfully come "just to check in." I was all bundled up in a cap and jacket, sitting under blankets, cold but too high to care much about it. That was why I spent whatever money I had on drugs. They sedated everything at once—the chills, the hunger, the remorse, the loneliness, and the general hopelessness. None of that came with you into the drug-induced state.

"How's school?" I'd ask, and she might not answer immediately. "It's fine." There was a catch in her voice, and if any light came through the window, or from a candle, it might have caught the deep concern in her eyes. She just couldn't stand what was happening to me, worst of all the idea of a wall between my parents and me.

"Go back to Mom and Dad," she'd say. "Just go back home and tell them you're sorry."

"I can't do that, Lori. I'm not wanted. Mom told me they never wanted to see me again."

"Come on, Robby, you know how she is. She gets angry, but she doesn't mean that. She and Dad are hurting badly over this. They're *missing* you. Just go home. Get some help. Look, Pawpaw's birthday is coming up in May. The whole family is getting together. You're not going to miss that, are you?"

I wouldn't talk about any of it, and Lori wouldn't stay long—she just couldn't take it, and I knew she'd be weeping before she made it to her car. But on the way out the door, she'd take my hand and I'd feel the folded rustle of cash. It would be a fifty or even a hundred. I knew she didn't have that kind of money, but she'd find it somewhere. She wanted to think maybe I'd get the heat turned back on, or the power. Or at the very least, get a meal.

Instead, of course, the money went into the hands of the local dealer. I wasn't evil. I wasn't apathetic. I was just completely enslaved by a master that never relented.

A couple of weeks passed by, then a couple of months—time didn't have a lot of meaning. But life had ingrained the New Orleans calendar in me, and I knew Mardi Gras was becoming a distant memory. Also, in the back of my mind was my grandfather's birthday—my whole family would be together, and I knew what my absence would mean. I felt a deep yearning to see them.

That's when Rodney showed up back in town from San Diego on one of his expeditions.

"Dude!" he said on the cellphone. "Are you ready to party?"

He described the new tattoo he'd just gotten inked on his arm. It was a scene of a dragon and a castle. "I can't wait for you to see it."

"I bet it looks amazing. Did you bring any—"

"You know it!" Rodney always came in town with no fewer than fifteen bottles of ketamine. Special K is a horse tranquilizer and, for people, a powerful hallucinogen.

I said, "It's going to be a weekend we won't forget. Where are we meeting?"

"Downtown, Dustin's apartment." Dustin was our cocaine connection. "I'm going to throw myself a welcome home party. Make sure you're there."

"Wouldn't miss it."

That night something came up. I was running late to the party—never made it, actually. I got a phone call on the way from Dustin. "Robby—Rodney's dead, man," he said.

"What? What did you say?"

"Rodney is dead." He was crying as he spoke. "Don't come here. We have to get rid of all this stuff immediately."

I knew the drill. Sadly, we'd been there before. Someone overdoses, you have to call the ambulance, and the police are going to be involved. It's a possible crime scene until everything is sorted out, so there's a lot of "evidence" to clean up. The detectives will be going over every corner, every inch with a fine-tooth comb.

After the call, I sat and thought about it. Rodney liked being high, but he wasn't reckless about it, like some. He had just started a new life, was finally happy. He was into some serious money. I heard what all was in his system, but Rodney knew how to pace himself through a party. It didn't sound like him.

What I also knew was that he had all those bottles, liquid gold. It was worth a whole lot of money on the street. Nobody seemed to be sure what had happened to all of his stuff during the "cleanup." And then I thought about the guy who hosted the party—a coke dealer, a guy who had nobody's complete trust. We called him *friend*, but that term was thrown around loosely. There was something shady about him—okay, there was something shady about all of us. But there were too many whispers about this guy. I had to wonder about his involvement in Rodney's death.

I also had to think, *This could have been me. Maybe should have been. Maybe will be, next time.* That's where my head was during those cold, hard seventy-five days.

Though I had my suspicion, the official word was that Rodney had been up for three days on crystal meth while traveling. He'd been using ketamine and cocaine. Whatever the details, his life was over. A little group of us went to the funeral home to pay our respects. We walked in quietly, through all the nice furniture and polite company. We signed the guest book, and we looked up to see our own faces in a photo collage—Rodney with his friends; Rodney as a happy child; Rodney with his family.

How does someone get from there to here?

In the parlor set aside for his loved ones, I wanted to see his body, to know it was really Rodney, my friend. It didn't seem real to me somehow. Somehow I got it in my mind that I needed to see the dragon and the castle on his arm. I wasn't thinking straight, of course; he was unlikely to be in that coffin in a short sleeve shirt. The mortician wouldn't have said, "Man, let's show off his tats!"

Still, I was making my way to the front when I saw there was no coffin. "He was cremated," somebody told us. And that was that.

For some reason, that really upset me. They burned his body to ashes before I could say my good-byes. Before I could get any closure.

Just then, somebody pointed at us and shouted, "Those boys! Those are the ones who killed my son!" And every eye in the room turned toward us, all these well-dressed church people glaring at a ragged band of junkies.

We pushed through the crowd. "Yeah, get out of here. You don't deserve to be here!"

We rushed to the parking lot and regrouped back at my place. Nobody could speak. We'd just been accused of contributing to the murder of somebody we deeply loved. And could there be some truth to that? Was his blood somehow on our hands?

We sat in the empty apartment, some of us on the floor, a wisp of light coming in through the shades, and we were quiet for a few minutes. Then my friend Rick said, "I'm getting clean. I'm telling you, I'm getting clean."

I said, "I'm in. Let's do it together, all of us."

"For Rodney."

Everybody said, "Yeah—for Rodney."

We meant every word of it, and I held to my convictions for two days. Until Dustin came over and said, "Listen, man, I know we're all hurting. Eight-ball of coke, on me."

I hesitated, for about two seconds. Three and a half grams of coke would cover lots of varieties of pain. And at the moment I was in a pretty good number of them. I said, "Come on in, Dustin."

Another half-serious attempt at coming clean was behind me. I found solace in the empty moments of bliss that followed.

From there, it's a blur, but I remember somehow my sister was back. Standing in my apartment, bag of groceries in hand, giving me an intense look.

"He's turning eighty," she was saying.

"Pawpaw," I said. I needed to focus.

"Yes. Pawpaw." She was after me again about going to my grandfather's birthday party. We loved him so much. He was a World War II veteran who owned a dairy farm for years—the Gallaty family patriarch. My father bore his name, then me. I'm Robert III. So Lori was laying the guilt on me in broad strokes—our Pawpaw was near the end of his life, and I was going to sit it out, leave a big empty spot at the celebration? Really?

"That's not fair," I said. "You know I can't go there."

"Of course you can go there. If you miss it, you'll never forgive yourself."

"I'm already never forgiving myself. Believe me."

She sighed heavily. "Come on, Robby. Please. Would you come just for me? I've never asked you for anything—just this one thing." The tears were about to come. I hated it, and I shut that conversation down. Stonewalled it—changed the subject—until she gave up and went out the door, hurt as usual.

I hated thinking of how much she worried about me. If time was running out for her grandfather, she had to wonder if the clock was running even faster on her brother, her only sibling. She would have done anything in the world to reach out and rescue me, whatever it took. But what could she do? Nothing in the world she could think of, other than to get me to a family party. It was the only weapon in her arsenal, and in the end, it hit the target.

Watching her leave, I was as upset as she was. I just couldn't let her see it.

Getting high affords you time to think, whether you want to or not. Your heart races too fast to go to sleep. Your mind never stops, so most nights are spent tossing and turning in bed.

I replayed every wrong choice I'd made. I relived the consequences of my actions. I thought often about my parents, wondered how they were doing and how angry they must be. One thing was certain: they weren't beating down my door, asking me to come home.

Maybe that's what I wanted—forgiveness without having to ask for it. I was the Prodigal Son demanding that his father come get him out of the pigpen. I think we all know, deep down, the story can't end that way.

I knew Mom and Dad so well that I could guess how they were taking all this. Mom was the key. She was the rock-solid foundation to our family, tough because she'd learned it was necessary. My mother had been around addiction all her life, and she had a perfect understanding of how things worked in that world. Her dad had been a drinker all his life. Her brother followed in his footsteps, dying early after a battle with alcoholism.

She knew all the signs, and she'd had her eye on me since I was little—my compulsive personality could quickly become an addictive one. As she watched me in all-out pursuit of basketball or music or DJing or anything else, she knew the potential for problems down the road. She understood my crazy passion was fine until I began to pursue the wrong things, which, of course, is what eventually happened.

I can remember going to the store with her as a child. "Mom, look at this toy truck! It's so awesome—can I have it?" I would beg and plead, trying to wear her down, and if she gave me a no, it meant *no*. I thought she was too tough, but in time I realized she was giving me exactly what I needed. There had to be solid boundaries when I was in hot pursuit, or I would chase something right over the nearest cliff.

We called Mom "The Warden"—even Dad said it. She physically threw me out of the house twice after arguments, and she didn't just look away and say, "Leave." She gathered up everything I owned and tossed it all out the door. Afterward, she'd soften around the edges and ask for forgiveness. She was great about that. But she'd grown up in an addictive household, she knew it was hereditary, and she understood that for some people, love must be tough or it isn't love at all.

Then there was Dad—the perfect complement to his wife. Dad was my mentor, my buddy, my role model in every way for what a man should be. He had a tough exterior but he was soft in the center. It wasn't coincidental that Mom had been the one to phone me about the $15,000. Dad didn't like confrontation unless it couldn't be avoided.

He had his own way of molding me. Dad always gave me tough tasks at the shop. He wanted me to learn what it meant to work a tough, grueling summer day with no air conditioning, getting grease under my fingernails and paint on my clothing. I needed to pay my dues, and the easy life could only come much later, after I'd earned it. We worked on cars together, played basketball, and functioned as friends every bit as much as father and son. But he wasn't the one to play the stern disciplinarian. I always knew his resolve would crumble, and he'd throw open his arms and say, "Let's just forget the whole thing."

Good cop, bad cop—a tried-and-true formula.

Mom understood that you couldn't just throw your arms open for the addict and ignore the issue. Addiction is a war, and it's not fought with pillows and warm hugs. Serious weaponry is required. So just about now, I figured, Dad would be saying, "C'mon, honey, let's drive over there and check on him. Let's make sure he's all right—maybe take him some food and mend fences. What do you say?"

And she'd be saying, "Nope. It doesn't work like that. He's done something terrible, there are consequences, and he has to get himself together. Then he can start mending fences with us."

Cold, unyielding, and a powerful expression of love that cuts through the blackest darkness. In the end, the tough love of my mother would save my life. I can't imagine how strong she had to be for that level of personal discipline. Because she loved me as deeply as any mother for her child, but she knew what I needed, and if she hadn't been there to give it, I wouldn't be here now.

———

The morning of the family party, I woke up with a clear grasp of what day it was. What's more, I knew I was going to go to the party. I hadn't gone to bed with anything resembling that conviction.

I have no idea what changed overnight. I just sat up in bed and knew. Some powerful impulse broke through just enough of my pride. I was able to tell myself I could go to the party and make an appearance. For Pawpaw's sake. No big deal. It didn't have to be a dramatic scene. Prodigal Dad didn't have to come sprinting down the road to embrace me. Just a drop-in, a hug for my grandfather. I could shower, make myself presentable, and take care of business.

When it was time, I snorted two Oxy-40s, showered in cold water, got myself dressed, and headed for the party. As

I walked up to the door, I could feel my heart beating. What did I think I was doing? It was too late to back down now.

I opened the door and there was my family—Mom, Dad, Lori, the others. Heads turned my way as I walked in. I put on a big smile and acted as if it were just another day. It was silent for a minute, then people resumed the laughter and conversation.

Mom walked over to where I was standing. I wasn't sure I could keep breathing. I could hear my heart pounding.

"Hello, Robby. How are you?"

Then I fell apart inside. It took all my strength to avoid melting down in front of Pawpaw and everyone else, but somehow I kept it all together. Mom could see what was going on inside me, though—she knew me too well.

"I'm not too good, Mom," I said.

"I know."

"I need help."

She nodded, and I saw the sadness in her, the worry-lines around her eyes, and I realized just how deep were my parents' wounds.

I couldn't hold in what I was feeling. With tears streaming down my cheeks, I said, "Mom—can I come to your house after the party?"

"Yes, Robby. Of course."

If I were the Prodigal, my long road wasn't about miles and distance. It was about finding three words. *I need help.* It was about coming to the end of myself and facing where I was. Pride is the last tower to fall.

With the help of OxyContin, I kept my composure for the rest of that celebration. I may not have been the life of the party; it was probably more than obvious I was no longer the Robby they knew. I was thin; I was quiet; I was somebody else wearing Robby's skin.

But I got through it, I followed my parents home, and there I humbled myself as deeply as I knew how. I got down on my knees before my mom and my dad. "Please help me," I said.

"Of course we will."

They welcomed me. They forgave me. And they told me they'd do everything in their power to rescue me from the mess I found myself in.

Chapter 10

COMING CLEAN

W here did it all go?"

My parents stood in the middle of my desolate apartment. They had once set me up in it, and they'd furnished it to make me comfortable. At one time this place had been filled with friends, refreshments, and festive banners congratulating me for my promising new career in the financial sector.

Now the unit was little more than a shell. I'd sold everything I could to keep the drugs coursing through my body.

"I'm sorry, Mom. Dad."

"You can't change the past. Just tell us where you took everything."

I brought my parents to the pawn shops, and piece by piece they bought back the things of mine that were still there—music gear, baseball cards, personal items. But there wasn't a need for furniture. The plan was to move me home, then figure out some way to get the drugs out of my system.

"You guys just need to understand," I said. "This is going to be hell on earth, getting me well. There's no easy way out."

I'd experienced withdrawals before. I'd run out of money, or the supplier would go dry. The body aches would

93

set in; there would be pain from head to toe; diarrhea, nausea, and stomach pains, not to mention the mental battle of wanting another hit. Long hours on the couch in a fetal position, incapacitated. Imagine the worst flu you've ever had. Multiply it by ten.

Symptoms would last five days, sometimes longer.

I had no idea what was going to be involved in a full detox. I'd never made it that far, but I'd never heard of any process that wasn't torturous. And would it even work? It's often said that traditional recovery approaches show no better than a 20-percent success rate.

So regardless of my parents' determination, I didn't feel much hope. I just knew I'd come to the end of the road. I was placing my life—what was left of it—in their hands.

Lori, with a sad smile, said, "Looks like you and me will be going through treatment together."

"What are you talking about?"

"While they're fixing you, they've decided to fix me, too—I've got to quit smoking."

I had to smile. Misery loves company. "The Warden's trying to lock both of us up," I said. We both laughed.

Our parents videotaped something off the TV about kicking the cigarette habit, figuring it would give them something to help Lori. But it was even more helpful than that. The show documented an alternative approach to treating drug addiction, involving NAD therapy—supposedly it was vastly more effective than the usual approaches. The catch was, this treatment wasn't available in the USA. Up to this time, it lacked approval by the Food and Drug Administration, so you had to go to Tijuana, Mexico, to get it. Apparently Tijuana was becoming quite the hub for alternative medical treatments of various kinds.

Mom and Dad liked what they heard on the TV special, but the irony of going to Tijuana wasn't lost on me. You flew into San Diego and crossed over to Mexico, just like my old friend Rodney had done. I thought about how he should have been here with me now, flying over there to turn his life around instead of to load up on more ketamine. Instead of getting high, I was going to get help.

"I don't know," I said. "Believe me, Tijuana is the very worst place to turn loose an addict like me."

"You won't be turned loose," my dad smiled. "Mom's going with you. The people at this clinic say, 'Bring somebody with you for support,' so you and Mom will have a little vacation, eat some Mexican food, and relax." He laid out the plan to fly over there four days from now, and I'd get ten days of IV transfusions.

"This has got to be costing some money," I said. "Over-the-border treatments won't be covered by your group policy. How are you paying for it? And how is Mom going to get off for two weeks?"

"Don't worry about any of that, Robby. This is your life we're talking about. You have one job, and it's to get well."

Best I could tell, the treatment would cost my parents about the same amount I'd stolen from them—doubling down on what I'd done to them financially. Years later I'd realize they were showing me a perfect model of the love and grace of God. I had inflicted the deepest kind of hurt on them, stealing from them and using the money to further wreck my life. Any other victim and I would have gone to prison.

I'd sinned against the very people on this planet who loved me the most, and now they were willing not only to take me in, but to uproot their lives and fork out that much more money to rescue me. How did they know I wouldn't just break their hearts again?

They didn't.

They just knew that love wouldn't let them give up on me.

At this point, no one in my family, least of all me, understood the spiritual concept of grace, as shown in Christ—yet somehow they lived it out. God took my family in his merciful hand and carried us forward.

The problem was, I was still an addict, and my body was still crying out for what it needed. There was no option of going "cold turkey," simply cutting off the flow of medication; I would have gotten very sick, very quickly. Mom and Dad called the clinic in Tijuana and came to understand there was nothing to do but buy some time with a few more pills until I could get to Mexico.

I needed four to five Oxy 40s a day just to maintain my habit, and my parents had to finance that at a hundred bucks per day. Drug dependency was awful, but I was used to that. Financial dependency on Mom and Dad for my habit, however—that was utterly humiliating. I didn't want them anywhere near the dealers and the transactions.

I told myself that if I could ever get clean, I was going to stay that way, if only for their sake.

I lined up a dealer and made the arrangements to get enough pills to hold me until the plane took off for Mexico—a maintenance dose. But I was so much in the grip of this addiction that I took more than I'd promised, of course. I'd take the next dose a little too soon. Or a lot too soon.

So the day we were supposed to take off, I saw I would run out of Oxys. That meant my inner clock was ticking. I had thirty-six hours, more or less, until I would be way too sick to fly or move for that matter.

Addicts live with constant fear of something happening to the dealer, or running out of money, or anything that could separate them from their dosage. It's utterly nerve-racking. So, approaching the time to fly out, I was a mess. I got on the phone and found a dealer, begged my mom for more money, after explaining I'd gone through the other stash too soon. Admitting that was one more humiliation, but by now they had a pretty good idea of my condition. No more "functioning addict."

It was thirty minutes until time to head to the airport, and I was screeching away in my car to buy drugs.

I met the supplier and got my Oxys. As I drove toward home, breathing a deep sigh of relief, I felt my car hesitate. The car lurched, and I realized my Mustang was out of gas. I had to pull over by the side of the road, with no time to fool with flagging someone down to get gas. I could fill the car up or make my flight. Not both.

I called my parents frantically, and there was nothing for them to do but hurry to where I was. Mom was going to drive with me to the airport, and Dad would stay back to get my car running again. They had to change all their plans on the spur of the moment.

I had no words. How much stress could I cause them? Did they have a limit?

We did board the plane, took off, and as we rose above the clouds, I told Mom, "Well, we've gotten through the *easy* part. Now all I have to do is defeat drug addiction." Mom didn't laugh, but then again, it wasn't very funny.

———

We landed in San Diego, crossed the border, and met some of the other people making the same recovery pilgrimage. I remember seeing this tall, blonde woman with her son, who was skinny, dead-eyed, clearly addicted. She was tense and anxious; he was damaged and beaten down. I realized that for everyone out there with my problem, several innocent bystanders surrounded them, people like this woman who was suffering helplessly, desperate to rescue someone she loved. And I wondered if my mom and I offered the same appearance.

The clinic was in a very ordinary, unimpressive building. It could have been the corner chiropractor's office. We stayed at a motel nearby, and we walked past all the local *farmacias* every day to get my treatment.

During the first morning, I met a guy named Carl, an addict who'd come by himself. I knew that broke the rule of "bring somebody with you." Carl and I started our regimens of IV treatments that lasted several hours. All it really took was patience—little sickness, no agony. Not a bad deal.

Dr. Hitt explained how drug abuse damages the neuroreceptors in the brain. I already had issues in that department as someone with ADHD. Dopamine is a neurotransmitter that regulates motivation, rewards, and pleasure. Do something satisfying and you get a happy little dopamine surge. People with certain kinds of neuroreceptor issues become sensation seekers. They're born, to some extent, with an addiction to positive stimulation. They chase the surge.

This is enough of a difficulty to live with on its own, but drug abuse takes all that and renders it a train wreck—it damages the neuroreceptors, and it creates a cycle of seeking the drug and needing it even more. Anyone can be an addict, but certain people are absolute walking targets for addiction. That was me.

After a consultation with the doctor, I knew I was in the right place. The success rate of his treatment was superior to any other treatment on the market. At the clinic, the nurses injected an amino-acid solution into my blood. The job of the aminos was to repair damaged proteins and help the damaged neuroreceptors rebuild in the right manner. To put it more simply, I was receiving intravenous treatments that fed my body's craving, but in a healthy way—which bought enough time for my body to get over its need for the *wrong* stimulation.

Within a couple of days, I could feel the difference. I was thinking clearly, the way I used to. I was feeling better, had a good appetite, and was alert.

Within three or four days, my mom told me she didn't recognize me. "Robby, you haven't looked this good in years," she said. "It's remarkable. But what's going to happen once we check out and go home? Are you going to go right out on the street and buy some more pills?"

"I don't think I will," I said. "I have no desire to. The cravings are gone." I felt stronger, but I wanted to be as honest as possible. "For now, Mom, it seems like I don't need that stuff anymore. But we'll just have to see how all of this holds up."

Mom nodded her head. She wanted to believe.

On the fifth day, the doctor asked me, "Robby, have you seen Carl?"

"Come to think of it, I haven't, Doc. Hasn't he shown up?"

"Nobody has seen him."

That evening we heard the news. Carl, who hadn't brought anyone to support him, had seen someone selling black tar heroin, something he'd always wanted to try. As I said, Tijuana has its dangers. In a moment of weakness, Carl had tried some—maybe he figured just a touch wouldn't do any harm. He couldn't have understood it undermined the entire, expensive, time-consuming treatment he'd come here for.

Carl was found beaten up, left by the road, and in no condition to continue. He had to be sent home.

I always wondered what happened to Carl. Was that his one shot at getting better, or was he able to raise the money all over again to come back to the clinic, or even recover some other way?

I realized how important it was to fend off that dangerous impulse, that "moment of weakness." No cure is foolproof, because we all play the fool; it just takes that one bad moment. I told myself I'd never be like Carl—I was too smart. Thinking that, of course, was the ultimate sign I wasn't smart enough. And it wouldn't be long before I, too, would play the fool.

After ten days of IVs, I couldn't believe how good I felt. Before heading home, we met with Dr. Hitt one final time. "I had forgotten what it was like to be well," I said. "It's only been two weeks, but that time already seems like a nightmare, something that didn't happen, and I just woke up."

"Recovery is like that for everyone," he said. "But don't relax too much. What we've dealt with is the physical element, and that's a big thing. Your body no longer craves that rush, which is great. You get a fresh start. But you know there's another issue, right?"

He tapped on the side of my head with a finger. "The mental part."

"Exactly. This is why we say, 'Once an addict, always an addict.' Whether it's alcohol, drugs, food, or anything else. The mind has to be retrained, not just the body. The body is more immediate, because there's pain, withdrawal, and all those symptoms. But your mind is what really counts in the long run. You're still going to have memories that float to the surface; moments when you think about the old highs and how they felt. Especially an ADHD guy like you. Carl had one of those moments in the middle of his treatment. You'll think, 'I could dull the pain right about now.' You'll remember it, you'll dwell on it, and saying no will just make it more seductive. Like saying you're never going to eat chocolate ice cream again. Ever. Now that I've said that, what does that do to the thought of ice cream?"

"Makes me want some right now."

"Exactly."

"So what am I supposed to do about this?"

"Talk to an addiction counselor. I'm sending you to Paula Norris, who isn't far from where you live. She'll walk you through weeks and months of reestablishing a healthy life. You need a better understanding of who you are and what makes you tick. Now listen—some people think they've crossed the goal line, the points are on the board, and they blow off their counselor. They say, 'I'm good from here. I can handle it.' But they can't, and they fall right back into the trap. Classic relapse. So my friend Paula will help you avoid that."

Paula had a practice in Slidell, Louisiana. Her clinic was familiar with the kind of treatment I had received, and she had a thorough understanding of addiction, as well as the challenges of being me. Over the next few months, she became not only a guide, but the kind of positive, supportive friend I desperately needed. Above all, she helped me understand myself for the first time.

Slidell is a forty-five-minute drive from New Orleans. I would sit and talk to Paula, and she wanted to know my whole life story. Like most people, she found it hard to believe.

"This stuff really happened to you? Just the way you're telling it?"

"I have no reason to make it up."

"Well, I'll tell you what I'm hearing. This is someone trying, from the first days of school onward, to be someone he isn't. The class clown. Then the one who does impersonations of all the teachers. Then the jock, the basketball star."

"I wanted to be good at something."

"You wanted to stand out. You were feeding on the acclaim, the attention. Not because you were egotistical, but because applause is the first powerful narcotic even kids can get their hands on. It releases that dopamine, your body's own in-house drug. The applause of the crowd is intoxicating, and you have to find new ways to get it, just like finding new drugs. But chasing crowd approval keeps you from being who you really are. One day you're the—what was it?—Brazilian jiujitsu guy. Then you're the club DJ. And the host of the Closer's Corner. Even the stockbroker. Who knows how many more hats you'd have tried on if drug abuse hadn't gotten in the way?"

I sighed. "I can see it. But who am I?"

"That's what you've got to find out. But in a healthy way. Robby, when you focus on something, you're powerful, productive—like a laser beam. The problem is that you've been pointing in the wrong direction for years. People with ADHD tend to be creative, effective, and successful once they figure out where to point that high-intensity beam. Before then, they point it in every direction, and a lot of people get burned. So let me give you this exercise as homework."

"I hate homework," I smiled.

"Well, you'll like this task, because you get to look at yourself in the mirror! I want you to wait until you're by yourself, then go to the mirror, put your nose right up against it, stare yourself down, and ask, 'Who is Robby Gallaty? What does Robby Gallaty want out of life?'"

"Okay, but I don't get it. How's this supposed to help? If the mirror talks back, I'll know I have mental problems."

"Just do it. See what happens. Answer your own question, when you have no one to impress and nothing to prove. Find out who you are when no one's looking."

I went home and tried it. First I felt a little silly. Then I began to think about that question and realized I had no answers at all. I was twenty-five years old, a guy with a crazy life, who had no idea who he was or what he wanted out of life.

That moment remains as one of the most difficult I've ever encountered—asking myself a question I couldn't answer. And maybe, just maybe it was a small beginning toward hearing the answer from Someone else.

Chapter 11

GET OUT OF TOWN

By the middle of May 2001, my head was spinning. But at least I was conscious of it. Maybe it's just that I was *using* my head for the first time in months.

Between last Thanksgiving and the end of spring, I'd walked a dark, terrible road through the world of addiction. I hadn't just taken drugs, but I'd sold them. I'd sold myself. I'd hurt my family. And I'd been right on the edge of having a criminal record—or something worse.

But May had come. In many cultures, the first of May is celebrated as the end of the winter. For us, it meant my grandfather's birthday, but it also marked the end of the coldest, most unforgiving winter of my life. I was feeling better and thinking about the future for the first time in a good while.

I truly believed I'd been set free, but that wasn't completely true. Dr. Hitt had mentioned the need not just for physical recovery but mental renewal. Now I know there's another component still—the spiritual component. And I still had no spiritual understanding of who I was or what my life should be. There was a deeper, even more serious addiction I still needed to break—a sin addiction—but at this point in my journey, I was deeply grateful just to be clean. I figured the worst was behind me.

Paula, my counselor, had helped me realize I had no idea who I was. I had spent my life trying to create an identity—trying different ones on like new clothes. But none of them had worked. I still needed to discover who I was.

Paula had one other strong recommendation: *Get out of town.* Start over somewhere else. Most addicts are tempted by one of three things: people, places, or things. I was tempted by all of them.

I wasn't sure what to think about the idea of leaving town. Why was everybody always trying to make me leave New Orleans? Rodney and Paula, for very different reasons, believed I needed new places, new faces. I think Paula understood how much of a chameleon I was, changing my colors to match the environment. I'd lived with Christians and gotten into a Christian band. I'd hung out in bars and become a DJ. I needed to be in the proper environment for healing.

She said, "Your enablers are all there in New Orleans. It will be far too easy to fall back into old patterns. It's like an alcoholic living upstairs from a bar."

"Yeah, I know. They're already calling me."

"Robby, what does the side view mirror on your car say? Ever read that little warning?"

"I think it says, 'Objects in mirror are closer than they appear.'"

"That's the one. Good advice. You need to put some distance between you and what's in your mirror. Because they're going to follow you. That's why you need to move. You can come back home in the future, but find a safe, quiet place for the present."

The only place I could think of was Mobile, Alabama, where my sister was attending college. Who better to keep an eye on me? And Lori said, to me and to our parents, "There are no drugs in Mobile. I haven't heard of anyone doing them. This place just doesn't have a lot of crime. You can move in with me on campus, then find a job somewhere around town."

I had no better ideas, so I packed the few things I needed and moved to Mobile for the summer of 2001. I slept on an air mattress on the floor of Lori's one-bedroom dorm room, on the South Alabama campus.

Mobile is a nice town with a lot of charm. It's on the Gulf, just like New Orleans, but the resemblance ends there. Nothing like Bourbon Street is to be found.

The first night I was in town, we unpacked my stuff and decided to go out and get a bite to eat. We walked into TGI Friday's to watch the NBA playoffs and took a seat at the bar. I wasn't about to order a drink; my instructions were to stay away from cigarettes and alcohol, because they were triggers for the old patterns I was leaving behind. Addicts often believe they can handle it, but stimulants like those provide a small spike to the nervous system, just enough to leave us wanting more. You don't want to awaken the beast.

I focused on the game on TV and chatted with the bartender. He seemed like a nice guy. I told him I was new in the area and looking for work. Toward the end of our meal, the bartender leaned across the bar and said, "I'm about to be on break. I'm gonna go smoke a joint. Want to come?"

"Um, I'll pass, but thanks."

I looked over at Lori, whose eyes were as wide as the plate in front of her. I worried she might start screaming at the guy, but he had walked away.

When we got to the car, I kidded her. "So, like you said, no drugs in Mobile, huh?"

"I think you're actually a magnet for drugs," she said. "You *must* be. I've been here three years, and nothing like that has ever happened to me. *Nothing* like that."

It was pretty strange. Was some invitation written on my forehead in ink visible only to other users, or what?

No, but later I learned that things are happening in the spiritual world, every moment of our lives. It's all on a frequency our senses don't pick up, but the Bible describes it clearly: spiritual warfare. As a nonbeliever, I had no clue about any of that. I did know that over the last few months, there had been times when I had somehow dodged disaster, against all odds. Other times, I'd been tugged toward the darkness by circumstances I dismissed as random. We all live on the front lines of a life-or-death conflict between good and evil. We're soldiers at war, all the while believing we're civilians. Some are cognizant of this battle. Most are not.

As we drove home, I talked with Lori about my future. I had to look for a job, and the pickings would be slim in Mobile. Most of my recent experiences were out of the question, including DJing in nightclubs—did this town even have any?

What Mobile did have was a few gyms, and it seemed it would be that, sell cars, or repair them. I ended up getting hired by Powerhouse Gym. With my size, of course, I was a pretty decent billboard for workouts, even being more than a little out of shape as I was by this time. But the manager at Powerhouse saw that I had good people skills, and he made me a sales consultant—the guy with the clipboard who takes you into the office and sells you on a membership. And of course I could work out for free. It wasn't a bad gig.

For several months, I lived quietly, staying busy, greeting people at the gym, restoring my own body, coming home, staying clean. Sometimes I'd shift my body on that hard floor, lying on an air mattress, and think about recent days, when I'd had the nice apartment uptown, the finest clothing, and everybody knew my name. I was the hit of the club scene. Now here I was, hustling memberships at the workout joint, living on the floor of a one-bedroom dorm room. Life has a way of humiliating you. Back at square one, once again, but at least I was in the game. I couldn't say the same for Rodney and a few other friends. Eight passed away from drug- or alcohol-related deaths. Six went to jail.

The summer passed, September began, and I remember one morning especially. It was the eleventh of the month. I drove in early, opened the gym for the morning shift, and greeted some of the regulars. We turned on the TV sets in front of the treadmills and bikes. The morning programs were interrupted with a report from New York City about a plane flying into a building—just awful. The World Trade Center. We turned up the volume and watched. I climbed on a treadmill and stared at the screen with everyone else as it happened again.

That second plane and second crash, of course, was the gut-punch to every American—the affirmation that we were actually under attack. No one in the gym spoke. You could just hear the whir of the machines, as people ran on the treadmills, pedaled their bikes, or worked the elliptical trainers.

A terrible day—one that turned life upside down in Mobile and everywhere else. What a reminder that there are bigger things going on in this world than my issues. Was war on the horizon? Could there be more attacks? For the first time in my memory, nobody knew what lay in our immediate future.

More and more I focused on the weight room, my latest all-out, ninety-to-nothing pursuit. When I worked out, I got into a zone. My past didn't exist. My body had the best, healthiest stimulation. Sweat was my new drug. There was nothing but the pure effort and exertion of getting stronger and fitter. The worst time of my life had come out of that accident and the injury to my back. The cure to the pain turned out to be worse than the disease. Now I was going to heal my aching back the right way—by exercising it.

I made friends with a guy who was a bodybuilder. "Listen, big guy," he said. "How'd you like to train with me? I can move you to the next level, lifting heavy. I could make you the powerhouse of Powerhouse Gym."

"Sounds good to me. Let's do it."

Bodybuilders focus on three exercises: the squat, the bench press, and the dead lift. The coach or trainer motivates, assists, checks your technique, and hopefully keeps you from killing yourself. There are plenty of other, more multifaceted forms of weight training, but muscle building is simple: put as many pounds into the air as you can.

One day in December, I was at the squat rack. In the squat, the barbell is below your traps and across your upper back. The movement is to get under the bar and push up. It trains most of the major muscle groups in the body, from the back, down to the hips, abdominals, and thighs. It's high reward, but like all weight training, high risk. I tweaked my back, and I felt it immediately, easing the weights down and groaning.

After the Mustang accident, which had hurt my back so badly, I'd now spent months building it back up, only to blow it out on one bad lift. I was beyond discouraged.

I talked with Lori about it. "I don't know any doctors here," I said. "The ones I know, in New Orleans, have got to be better than here."

"And they'll give you pain meds."

"Well, they may, but I won't take anything unless I have to. Then I'll just sell them. Don't you think I've learned my lesson by now? I'm not getting hooked on that stuff again."

She gave me a doubtful look. "Are you going to talk with Paula about this? What do you think she'll say?"

I dodged that one. "No need for this to be a big deal. I'll just go for a checkup. We'll see what happens. Like I said, I'll sell the pills."

"To all your old buddies," Lori said. "Just great." She pulled out a cigarette. When she was nervous, she smoked. "If you get back into that life, Robby, I'll go ahead and kill you myself, get it over with."

———

NB

This was the addiction talking, of course. No matter how clean you get, the beast is still somewhere inside you, clawing to get out. It speaks through your bravado. It tells you, hey, you've got this. You're indestructible. You can dip your toe in the water and pull it right back out, man.

And of course, none of that is true.

I really believed I wasn't going to "start back." But it doesn't work that way; you never "start back"; you pick up where you left off. There's a huge difference. Picking up where you left off isn't gradual. You take the same dosage of drugs that you were taking before you got clean. You don't ease your way back into it. You suddenly find you're in completely over your head, right where you were drowning the last time. Just as helpless.

With substance abuse, there's no "dipping a toe in the water." That metaphor doesn't apply. If you're in at all, you're in deep.

I didn't know any of that, somehow. I headed to the doctor, whom I hadn't seen in eight months. He did the X-rays, checked out my back, and of course, sent me home with Oxycontin, Valium, Percocet, and Soma. I went to the pharmacy, filled my prescription, and stared for a moment at the innocuous little pill container. An old, familiar friend.

I had every intention of keeping the pills just in case, then selling them. But then I thought, *I might as well take one. Just one. See how I do.*

Which is always how it starts. Toe in the water, then you're drowning.

I took the pill, closed my eyes, and the effects slowly began to set in—wonderful and terrible. There was the surge I'd secretly craved for months. I'd forgotten how good it felt. I think I knew, whether I admitted to myself or not, that there was no turning back.

Nor did my back improve. It only got worse. In March 2002, I was scheduled for discectomy surgery on L5-S1 in my lower back, to shave away the part of the disk causing the pain. This diagnosis had a dramatic effect on my still pending legal complaint. Facing surgery, and all those months of pain—I had quite the case now: personal injury, pain, and suffering, with all the evidence on my side.

The lawyer advised me to go ahead with the surgery. My case had moved from a small claim to a $300,000 lawsuit. "Robby, the company is going to pay for your surgery, rehab, and some compensation for everything they've put you through."

I couldn't believe it. I figured my days of sleeping on the floor were over. If I was careful with that money, after my surgery, I'd have a head start on a brand-new life. I'd have to wait for the company to come up with a settlement, but in the meantime, I would receive $3,000 advance checks monthly.

The first check arrived just before I went into the hospital, and of course my addiction reared its ugly head immediately. I blew the whole thing on drugs. I told myself I needed relief from the pain, but it was all about the addiction. I realized it, but I didn't have much time to think about it when the surgery happened—the operation was like having a ton of bricks dumped on me.

After I came out, I couldn't feel my legs at first, so I couldn't walk. I had to wear a body brace and do lots of painful therapy. I began supplementing my drugs with hard liquor, which I could find in the house; I was back with my parents, sleeping in a rollaway bed in their living room. I was told to stay put, rather than going to the doctor for personal therapy.

I don't like lying around, particularly when I'm in pain. My spirits were pretty low, but some of my old friends, my partying buddies, were there to cheer me up. They were really glad to have me back in town.

I gave my friend Elliot a call. He said, "Robby! Hear you're back in the game again."

"Not completely. I'm laid up after a back operation, trying to get on my feet."

"So I hear. You'll be needing some party time to get your mind off things . . ."

"Yes, I will. And I've got a little money. Or I'm about to have some. That's why I need your help."

"Oh, yeah! I'm on it."

"My next check is due—three-K. You think you could go grab it for me?"

"I'm your guy." I could imagine him all but drooling over the thought of all that money for drugs. I told him where to go, but he called me back and told me the lawyer wouldn't release the check to just anyone. I had to sign for it. I told him to come pick me up, we'd get the check, and then we could stop off at The Pimp's place and stock up.

That's how he was known: The Pimp. He lived in the heart of New Orleans, and he was very careful about his business associates. He had to know you pretty well to build some trust, then he would supply cocaine and heroin, or "boy and girl," as we called it on the streets. The coke came in plastic bags. The heroin in tin foil, rolled into tiny squares.

Elliot helped me into his grandfather's single cab S10 pickup truck, body brace and all. It wasn't comfortable, but relief was a cashed check away. We drove past Canal Street to my lawyer's office, and I picked up my check. I cashed it at the Regions Bank around the corner as quickly as possible, then we paged the Pimp to let him know we were set. He met us on a side street. Elliot, as he always did, jumped out of the truck. Five minutes later, we were cruising back home with an eight ball of coke and two hundred dollars' worth of heroin foils. I figured if it was up to me, I'd feel no pain during my recovery. And with my current income, it would be up to me for the foreseeable future.

This became my ritual once a month, when I'd snort my way through three thousand dollars. We wouldn't even wait until we arrived somewhere—we'd start the party right there in the truck, dumping out the powder on CD cases, cutting lines of coke with a credit card before snorting.

We headed home down Canal Street toward St. Claude Avenue. As we sat at a traffic light, I looked out the window at a police station on Rampart Avenue as we passed it on our way back to Chalmette. Elliot was driving his grandfather's truck, while my bulky frame, still in the brace, was stuffed into the passenger side, and I was holding four hundred dollars' worth of drugs, ready for consumption. Right behind us, a car lit up like a Christmas tree: unmarked squad car.

"Where in the world did he come from?" I blurted out.

"No idea," said Elliot.

We pulled immediately over to the curb. I intended to stuff the baggies into my sock, but two officers yanked open our doors and ripped us out of the truck before Elliot could put the vehicle in park. At the very last second, as my door was flung open, I tossed the drugs under my seat.

The officer threw me against the side of the vehicle, body brace and all. As I was held there, his companion began searching the vehicle. He looked under the driver's seat, he went through the compartments in the door, and he checked in the glove compartment. Elliot and I were thinking, *Here it is—Possession with Intent to Distribute.*

What would my sentence look like? I had a clean record and came from a good family, but I'd still be looking at several years. I could cut the sentence down by flipping on some of our suppliers, of course. And never live in New Orleans again. I thought about my parents. They believed I was at home laid up in bed right now.

Suddenly, without more than a quick thought, I lifted my shirt and showed where I'd had surgery. "Please don't hurt me," I shouted. "I've just had surgery, I'm in the midst of a lawsuit, and my friend here is taking me home."

The officer walked up to me, looked me over carefully, nodded, and said, "You guys can go."

What? It worked?

We nodded, climbed back into the truck, and watched the unmarked car pull around us and drive away. I took a deep breath, but neither of us could speak for a few minutes.

We were trembling. I looked at my feet and saw the drugs poking out beneath the seat, in plain sight. How could an experienced officer miss them?

"Elliot. Look at my feet."

He gawked for a second, his mouth wide, and punched me in the shoulder. "You idiot!" he said. He used more colorful terminology. "Why didn't you put it in your sock?"

"I couldn't. I didn't have a chance."

He just stared at me, but his anger quickly receded. "Well, I can't get mad at you," he said. "Because I ought to mention—I don't have a driver's license."

I glared back at him. "You idiot!" And I punched him in the shoulder.

"I'm driving on a traffic ticket," he explained. "They took my license in New Mexico for possession of marijuana."

How did they not check his license? It's Traffic Stop 101, Police Academy, first year. If they'd just done that, we'd have both gone to the station. Then, after a more thorough search, we'd have been locked up for a long time.

They'd missed the license. Then they'd missed the drugs. What are the chances of both happening?

Even the way I was, even with my epic ignorance, I had a stray thought. *Somebody's watching out for me. There's no other way to explain it.*

Then the thought escaped me. I snorted another line.

Chapter 12

MADE NEW

One step forward, two steps back.

After several months of being clean and healthy, I was back on drugs and in way over my head. But this time there was a new twist—I was financed by a legal settlement. At the worst possible time, I was getting monthly checks that required nothing from me but retrieving and endorsing them. So I had all the money I needed and a terrible way to make it vanish.

This went on from March to October of 2002. I was miserable. Meanwhile, I had a vague awareness that our nation wasn't doing too well, either. The USA was coming to terms with a brand-new kind of war: one against terrorism. We were gearing up for war. The stock market took a roller coaster ride.

For a while there, I'd been in Mobile, quietly rebuilding my life. But I picked up right where I'd left off in New Orleans. I worked in my dad's shop and did my best impression of a drug-free personality. I could be pretty convincing; I'd learned how to live two lives.

One Thursday night I was on the way home after playing pool with a few buddies at Buffalo's Billiards. With me in the car was a nice supply of coke I'd scored at the pool hall.

The night was dark and quiet. I had a normal route I used for driving home, making a turn onto a side street to beat the traffic light. I'd gone that way hundreds of times since I was sixteen. As I took a left, I caught a glimpse, out of the corner of my eye, of a guy in the grass. My vague impression was that he was probably homeless, the type you'd see out late at night wandering around town. I recall there were papers in his hand.

Suddenly he moved sharply into my field of vision, onto my right front fender. He had to have moved pretty quickly to get there. I didn't feel any real impact, but I could see that his papers shot straight up in the air while he fell to the ground. I braked quickly as I watched the final page drifting to the pavement.

I pulled up a few feet, opened my door, and stuck my head out to see if he was okay. The man scampered up and let out a torrent of cursing and fist shaking in my direction, but he didn't look injured in any way—at least not judging from his movements.

The right thing to do was to call the police and report it. Then I thought about the cocaine in my car. I closed my door and stomped on the gas pedal to get out of there.

I was thinking there was no way this wasn't a setup. He'd been standing there by the curb, waiting for me to pass by, and at the very last second, he'd thrown himself onto the side of my vehicle—not enough to get really hurt, but sufficient to set himself up as a victim.

I wasn't going to be set up by this guy. No, I'd race home, lie low, and take my chances.

Which was a mistake, of course. The *smart* play (from the point of view of someone as lost as me at that time) would have been to ditch the drug discreetly and wait for the police to show up. I was neither smart nor honest in those days. I took a few back streets, pulled into our driveway, and walked through the house. I didn't say a word to my parents, but I'll admit to a pretty poor night of sleep that evening, with or without the assistance of medication.

The next day I went to work as usual. During the lunch break, I was out in my car and on my way home, about to execute a turn from the middle lane, when I looked in the rearview mirror and saw, to my alarm, that a police officer wanted me to pull over. Maybe my turn signal was out. Maybe it  was something trivial. I could only hope it wasn't about the previous night.

Immediately two policemen confronted me.

"Sir, was your car involved in a hit-and-run last night?"

So much for "trivial."

"No, sir."

They were watching my eyes, the way officers do. "We have a positive ID on a red Mustang, just like yours, sir. From last night."

"Sir, it couldn't have been me. I was at home all evening. I live with my parents—they'll tell you I was there."

The officer gave a noncommittal nod and handed me a card. "Robby, this investigator will come see you at five o'clock today. You need to be at home waiting for him to interview you."

As I climbed back into my car, a little shaken, I realized I needed to bring my dad up to speed on this one. And I really didn't look forward to that. Back at work, I sat down with Dad and told him what had happened—how I was certain it was a setup, and the guy didn't seem hurt at all.

Dad sighed unhappily, thought it over, and said, "Son, you need to deny the whole thing. You don't want something like this to escalate into a big mess. Late night, nobody around—it's just going to be your word against his."

If all of these things happened today, of course, I'd handle it with full integrity, and so would Dad. But at this moment in 2002, we were willing to cut corners—anything to avoid the judgment and exposure that I subconsciously feared would one day come.

I was on my way home at four, and I decided to stop by the Sno-Ball stand. This is a New Orleans specialty, shaved ice with cane syrup. I stood in line and placed my order. Six or seven people were standing behind me. The place was always packed. Suddenly a police car pulled up at the stand, then another one. Then it became clear something was going on with the police. A voice came from a megaphone: "Mr. Gallaty, please step away from the stand and walk toward this vehicle."

Everyone turned to look at me.

Several policemen surrounded me and began firing questions at me. "Did you hit a pedestrian? Were you out that night in this car?" I vehemently insisted that I hadn't done it. I'd been home. My parents were with me, and they'd swear to it.

"Son, we know the truth. You need to go ahead and confess, or you're going to jail."

"I didn't do it!"

I was placed in handcuffs. The officer said, "Okay, then, here's what we're going to do. We need you to stand here by this car facing the street. Two sets of witnesses will drive by and take a look at you. If they positively ID you, you're going to jail. Is that understood?"

"Yes, sir." Apparently, there was someone who watched the accident happen. Or claimed to be watching.

The first car drove by slowly. It had tinted windows to protect the witness. A police radio nearby crackled, and I heard the words, "He says that's him."

The officer got in my face and said, "Son, one more to go. If he says yes, you'll be under arrest."

Just then yet another police car pulled up—and a friend stepped out. It was a buddy of mine who was an officer. He said, "I know Mr. Gallaty. Let me have him for a minute."

The others stepped aside, and my friend said, "Dude— what are you doing? You're sending yourself to jail. They totally know you did this. Just admit it and take a ticket. Then it's a civil matter between you and the guy, see? So take the ticket, sleep in your own bed tonight, and let your insurance handle it, instead of turning it into a law enforcement matter. Because, let me tell you: it's Friday afternoon. You check in tonight, you'll be in custody all weekend."

I realized how clueless I was about this stuff. I quickly told the other policeman I was ready to admit to the incident. I took my ticket, drove home, and explained the situation to my parents. And the "victim" went on to sue the insurance company. It turned out I was right about his motives. He'd tried the same thing twice already, stepping in front of cars and cashing in on settlements. This time, he received a small check. I could have fought it, but I had other battles in my life.

The real news was that I'd dodged a larger bullet, and I knew it. If I'd been caught with drugs in my car—on either day—there would have been no escaping a serious arrest.

For a little while longer, I continued to beat the odds. And when I thought about it, I realized it was very odd indeed.

I was miserable. I was deceiving my parents again. I'd escaped the prison I'd sentenced myself to, only to lock myself up again.

Maybe I didn't deserve a break.

I couldn't see any way out. The NAD treatment was expensive, and I couldn't stand the shame of asking for help. Not a second time.

One of the problems with nearly any kind of addiction is that your needs escalate. In the case of drugs, your system builds up a tolerance to the old dosage; it calls for a larger amount. In my case, I was supplementing drugs with alcohol, almost a fifth of Jack Daniels a day. The rest of the time I was going through one cigarette after another. At one point, I was smoking two and a half packs a day. My system was demanding any little spike it could get, and I was slave to those demands.

My parents kept alcohol in their closet, and during those two months at home, I'd go in, drink the bottle, and replace the whiskey with water, so it wouldn't look empty. Obviously this wasn't going to work forever, but addicts never worry about tomorrow. They don't have that luxury.

———

During the summer, Dad surprised Mom and took her on a trip to Europe. Talk about a well-deserved break. He left me in charge of the shop, and I continued to drink, take drugs, and wonder how low I could sink.

The day came when my parents returned. Not long afterward, Mom went into the closet, reached for a bottle, and found it filled with water. Then another bottle. Then another. Once again, the whole truth dawned on her. She was furious with me and dumbfounded that she and my dad had been fooled again. Knowing I was back on drugs, they were both furious and heartbroken, and I was even more furious and more heartbroken with myself.

Like I said, 2002 wasn't a happy year for anybody.

Once I got to the middle of October, I realized I was at the breaking point. Fed up. No longer willing to put up with another day of this misery. The confrontation with my parents, whom I've always loved so deeply, broke through the haze of drugs and alcohol and made me face the truth. I was broken. I had failed, been rescued, then failed again. The shame was unbearable.

Frankly I wasn't sure whether my life was worth continuing. I thought about suicide. As I lay awake, I would think about the eight friends who had already died to alcohol- or drug-related deaths. Some died by car accidents, others by overdoses, and one by suicide. Any night could have been my last, given the amount of drugs I was consuming. I was one bad batch away from a grave myself.

I thought about all of this and came to the decision that life would go on, but I had to detox myself. I knew that a trip to Tijuana was no longer necessary for the amino acid treatment. I could have it done at Paula's clinic in Slidell, not far from home—it was now approved for the United States. And Paula said I didn't need the full ten days of treatments. A three-day tweak, she believed, would get it done, and I'd be free again.

I told Paula I was going to get that tweak soon; then I went home with a plan of my own. No way I was going to let myself off cheaply. I was sick and tired of being sick and tired. The NAD treatment wasn't punishing enough. The way I saw it, I'd done something terrible, I'd hurt my family, and I needed to pay.

If there was one thing I could understand, it was that sin demanded payment. That's why I was going to detox myself and take the full burden of my wrongdoing.

I spent a week starving my system of those spikes it demanded. No drugs. No alcohol. No matter what. It was just as terrible as I knew it would be, and then some. This was the only way I felt I could really get clean—making it hurt.

I realize now there was an element of self-loathing and masochism, but that's where my head was in those days. There were about ten days of projectile vomiting and diarrhea; I was sick to my stomach and in despair of life. The human body wasn't meant to endure that kind of pain.

Worst of all, my parents had to watch. What could they do? I told them they couldn't interfere—I'd brought this on myself and I shouldn't be let off the hook. Today, as a parent myself, I can't begin to imagine what it's like to watch one of your own children suffer like this.

Finally the symptoms began to subside, my body got the message that no more drugs were coming, and the cravings leveled off. I felt the peace that comes after the storm, but no real sense of joy or fulfillment. Just emptiness.

My body may have been free, but I still had no identity. *Who was Robby Gallaty?*

On November 11, I drove to Slidell to receive treatment from Paula's clinic, just to finish off the job and restore my system. I went again for the second of three days and reflected on the fact that I wasn't feeling any better about any of it. I'd gritted out a detox, all by myself, and I should have felt the taste of victory, or even just a powerful sense of relief. I should have felt hopeful, if humbled.

But all I felt was desolation.

I had to admit it wasn't just about drugs. Paula had been talking to me about all those roles I'd played, all those fake identities: Robby the basketball player, Robby the stockbroker, Robby the entertainer, Robby the magician. I was still looking in the mirror and seeing . . . nothing.

I walked into our home that evening, had dinner with my parents, and went quietly to my room. At bedtime I couldn't sleep, as usual. I hadn't had a good night's sleep for at least ten days. Something was getting under my skin, and at some point, I began to realize it was God.

He was calling out to me, demanding my attention. It was something like becoming aware of distant music that was there all along, part of the background noise. Then you stopped and took notice.

It happened for me because he had been on my mind lately. During the worst of my addiction, I'd fear for my life. I'd cry out to him, "Don't send me to hell!" For me, God was merely the judge who rapped the gavel and declared your sentence, frown on his face. I viewed him as an authoritarian dictator out to chastise me every time I got out of line. That and nothing more.

Now I knew he was someone who spoke—someone trying and trying to get through to me. He'd been doing it—well, maybe all my life. I just hadn't stopped, tuned in, and let his voice come through. I'd been in too much of a hurry, too self-involved. If I didn't know who I was, how could I know who he was?

If he wanted so badly to get through to me, maybe he was more than a gavel-pounder. I wanted to know his message now—*really* know it.

I felt him pouring all kinds of thoughts and feelings into my mind. He made me see my life for what it was. I was absolutely incapable of living the way I should, and *sin has consequences*—I believed that. I'd tried to carry the burden of my own sin through detox. But now I knew it was about more than the drugs in my system. It was about a deeper burden, one I couldn't carry.

Jeremy Brown, my old friend from college, came into my mind—Jeremy, who had loved me as a friend, then shared his faith with me in a way that actually made sense. Jeremy knew how to hear God's voice. I'd tried to imitate his actions, but I hadn't known his Lord. I couldn't, because I had no conception of my sin in those days.

Now I was broken. I knew what it meant to be overwhelmed by the darkness of my own heart. I had nothing to fall back on in this world, no place to find hope.

Jeremy had asked me to pray with him, phrase by phrase, and he'd helped me understand what I was saying to God. But this was different—I was crying out in pain from the depth of my soul. My attitude with Jeremy had been, "Sure, okay, I'll try this thing." Back then, Jesus was an addition to my life, just one more color in the spectrum. He never became my life. Now I was utterly lost, desperate. Jeremy had said all of us are sinners, all of us are unworthy, and finally I *felt* the meaning of that. I *owned* it. And that was the greatest difference.

Ever since that accident with my Mustang, when everything began to go wrong, I'd pointed my finger elsewhere. I'd blamed circumstances. I'd said, "If only this or that hadn't happened, I'd have it all together right now; if only this person hadn't done that, I'd have been fine."

The blame game didn't work for me now. I owned my sinfulness, and because of that I experienced God as real, as a person and not a concept or abstraction. He was calling me home.

He seemed more real than anything in the world at that moment. He was a loving Father who wouldn't give up on me, who would go to any length to rescue me. I thought of my parents, watching me suffer through detox, wishing they could take my pain for me.

Hadn't God done something like that? Hadn't he taken my pain? Didn't he let his Son carry my burden on the cross?

I let the tears flow as I thought about the idea of him loving me that much. Why had I only seen him as an angry judge?

For the next twenty-four hours, I wept, I prayed, I owned my wretchedness, and I called out to God. I told him that Stockbroker Robby wasn't good enough; DJ Robby and Jiu-Jitsu Robby weren't good enough; none of the Robbys were good enough.

If I understood this thing correctly, only Jesus was good enough. I had detoxed myself, carrying the burden of my drug addiction. I suffered, I made it through, but Detox Robby wasn't good enough, either. I'd felt nothing but emptiness at the end of it all. Only Jesus could carry that burden, and he carried it on the cross. For the first time, I realized it was *my* sin that Jesus bore on the cross.

So many of Jeremy's explanations came back to me now, as if they'd been seeds planted in hard ground and were just now finally breaking through the dry soil of my understanding.

The only other thing I can tell you about that night is that it was a highly supernatural experience. I think I felt like the apostle Paul may have when he described Jesus showing him the third heaven (2 Cor. 12:2–4). It was just for me, so words will not convey what took place.

For every one of God's children, it will be different. I only knew he had invaded my life, once and for all, and that nothing could ever be the same again.

I must have dozed off at five in the morning, and when I woke up, a few hours later, I realized everything was different. My emptiness had been filled to the brim, and joy was flowing over the sides.

Immediately I had the idea to write down my prayers, to journal them, and I recorded them furiously, almost scratching through the paper with my pen. The words that were swirling in my mind were *Be still and trust in me*. It was only later that I came across Psalm 46:10, "Be still, and know that I am God" (ESV). I'm sure I'd never heard those words before, but now they came to me and filled me and molded me. I was the least "still" person I knew. My mantra had been, "If it's meant to be, it's up to me." On a scale of 1 to 10, I'd gone after everything at 11.

But now God was telling me, "Stop. Just stop. *You be still* and trust me." It was indeed meant to be, but it was up to *him*. I felt he was teaching me dependence, faith, and the idea of abiding in him, though *abiding* was another concept I hadn't yet discovered.

Looking back, I realize I was abounding in ignorance. But the Spirit of God was with me now, and finally I felt the wind at my back.

———

Drugs were never my problem; drugs were only the symptom. Ultimately, there's one true addiction and only one path to breaking free from it.

In John 8, Jesus told a group of people that anyone who sins is a slave to sin. But "if the Son sets you free, you really will be free" (v. 36). I had been a slave to sin. Sin was the problem. And I needed more than detox. I needed the Son of God, Jesus Christ, to set me free.

And now, he had.

I believed I had broken through, or more precisely, someone had broken through on my behalf. God did for me what I was incapable of doing for myself. He set me free from the bondage that had shackled me for years.

That bright morning I walked into the kitchen with a big smile on my face, and there was Dad, sitting at the breakfast table. He looked up and said, "What are you so happy about?"

"God is calling me into the ministry to be a preacher, Dad!"

I was a bit surprised to hear those words come out of my mouth, but I realized that, yes, this *was* what I was feeling. This wasn't just about being a believer—God had specific plans for me. I was sure of that. When you've had a burning bush experience like I'd just had, you have to do something with it. Silence is not an option.

Dad studied me for a moment, trying to figure out if I was still on drugs, but he saw that I was dead serious. His brow wrinkled and he said, "You're going to be a priest? How will you ever get married, if you do that?"

"No, Dad," I laughed. "Not a priest. A preacher!"

I realized he had no frame of reference for what I was talking about. In the Catholic environment I grew up in, crazy, Road-to-Damascus conversions weren't typical. There were priests on a pedestal above, and then there was everybody else.

It would be a while before Dad really grasped what I was talking about, before he saw that his son had been set on fire.

Somehow I was going to be a preacher. God had stuff for me to do. Time to go figure out what it was.

Chapter 13

BABY STEPS

The day after I committed my life to Jesus, I found my Bible on the shelf, dusted it off, and sat down to read it with new eyes.

I thumbed through the huge volume. There were hundreds of pages of tiny print, made up of smaller books with names like *Leviticus* and *Lamentations*, *Obadiah* and *Ephesians*. History, psalms, prophesies—where was the section for beginners?

I thought about the songs I'd learned in our Christian band, back in my college days. I could remember all the words, but they didn't offer much guidance to a new believer. I prayed, but I wasn't even sure how to do that. My go-to prayer had been, "Please don't send me to hell." Even I knew there was more to it than that.

What should I say to God? How would I hear what he said to me?

I guess most of all I needed someone to talk to about the whole thing. My life felt different, but I didn't know any truly committed followers of Jesus. I had lots of energy and lots of questions. Still, I knew I was at peace, filled with hope, and deeply grateful to be forgiven. The turmoil and desperation were gone, and it felt like the quiet after a storm. It was time to reboot my life.

I had to start with what I knew for sure: My old lifestyle was done—finished. My old friends would encourage my old habits. Besides, once drugs were taken out of the equation, what did I really have in common with that crowd? Not much. I'd even dumped my whole music collection in the trash.

My old friends began to call, one by one. They'd heard the rumor, but they wanted to hear it from me. Word on the street was that I'd had some freaky conversion experience. I wasn't Robby anymore—at least the Robby they knew.

"It's true. I accepted Christ," I told my friend Rick. "My life is completely changed, and God is calling me into the ministry."

"Really, Robby? You, of all people, a Jesus freak? You can't be serious."

"Absolutely."

"Robby, we never had a question about who you were. You had our trust. This is nuts."

"You can still trust me, Rick. I'm *more* trustworthy now. I'm just no longer interested in getting high."

"Couple of guys are saying you've turned informant. That you're an undercover cop. You gonna rat us out?'"

"You know better than that, Rick. I wouldn't hurt my friends—not in a million years. You guys are family to me. Don't you remember all those times we talked about getting clean? I've done it now, that's all. I'd love for all you guys to do it, too, but I'm no cop, and I've talked to no cops. You've got my word on that."

Conversations like this went on and on with different friends. I wasn't trusted now, and maybe that was for the best. My bridges were burned to the ground. As a new Christian, I was on an island.

Most people become Christians in some kind of social context. Friends lead them to Christ, as Jeremy had once tried to do with me. But I was all by myself when God broke through.

For about two weeks, I read my Bible the best I could, and now I knew what to pray for: "God, send me somebody. Give me a guide to help me walk this new path." I knew I needed to be involved in a church, but it had to be the kind where believers were excited and alive. There were scores of churches around, so I had no idea where to go.

Then one day I got a call from Julie, right out of the blue. She was one of a group of four girls who were my close friends during our college days. We hadn't talked since then.

"Hey, Robby!" she said. "Are you still alive?"

"Looks that way," I laughed. "It's great to hear from you, Julie. Any reason I shouldn't be alive?"

"Yeah, based on the way you were going at Carey. We wondered how long you were going to last."

"You were right. And it got worse." I told her about the car wreck, my addiction, my trips to rehab. It was much worse than she knew, but all that craziness was behind me.

"I dug myself as deep a hole as you can dig. . . . Then I found Jesus, just in the last few weeks. And actually he's calling me into the ministry."

Julie shouted into the phone, "What?"

"I said I've—"

"I heard what you said! But, I mean—*what*? We've been praying for you. So I don't know why I'm so surprised. It's just—so awesome! And lately, I've just had this strong feeling I needed to call you."

"And I've been praying you'd call me—you or somebody who could tell me what to do."

"Well, come to our Bible study, Robby! That's what you should do. You'll love it! I'll hook you up with a bunch of other people who really love God, especially T-Bone. He can answer all your questions."

I knew a lot of T-Bones—none of them were guys I thought could teach me about Jesus. But God had more surprises around the corner for me.

———

I showed up on the campus of the University of New Orleans to study the Bible. Julie met me there and introduced me to this guy named Tony Merida, who was a little short of a T-bone in physical stature—more like a sirloin steak. But in every other way, this guy was a beast.

When we sat down to study the Bible, Tony began to teach those chapters and verses in a way I didn't even know was possible. The pages of my Bible came to life.

This was nothing like the cut-and-dried religion I knew from childhood. It was all about real life, daily decisions, getting along with other people, handling the problem of sin, and how to connect with God in the midst of all this. I was spellbound for an hour.

After it was over, T-Bone said, "Hey, man, can I invite you to my church?" It took me about one second to accept. Like most new believers, I was ravenous for knowledge and guidance, and I knew he and I were going to become good friends.

His church was called Edgewater Baptist Church. I pulled into the parking lot on the following Sunday, dressed exactly the way I was used to walking into nightclubs: black pants, black shirt, hair slicked back with lots of hairspray and gel. So here came a six-six gangster into the sanctuary. I imagine some of the deacons were keeping an eye on me when the offering plate went around.

I began to grow through fellowship with other Christians and Bible study, but something else happened. Just about then our case was finally settled in court, and we won. I'd been receiving preliminary monthly payments, but now I was awarded a $150,000 check. Now I wasn't only a Christian—I was a rich Christian. And the first thing I did was to hurry over to the Cadillac showroom and buy a brand-new Caddy, with cash. Black on black was my choice. I had the car fully customized.

I lowered my new CTS to the ground, installed 20-inch chrome Katana rims and tires, Borla exhaust, body kit, spoiler, wood grain trim, and a $9,000 custom stereo system. No one had seen anything like it, since it was hot off the assembly line. With my modifications, it looked like the Batmobile—at least that's what people called it.

Baby Christians take baby steps. It's been proven over and over. They're excited, eager, and not quite as far along the path of maturity as they think. They tend to see everything that happens as a text message from heaven. For example, I figured that if I immediately received a huge sum of cash, right after becoming a Christian, it could only be a massive high-five from the Lord.

I was new at this thing. It would never have occurred to me that money isn't always a blessing. It's more likely to be a test. It certainly was in my case.

It was a lifelong dream to own a brand-new Cadillac, but the way I saw it, why couldn't it be a four-wheel billboard for God? I could drive around town, attract a lot of eyeballs, and say, "Look what God has done in my life, folks!"

Me and God—together, there was nothing the two of us couldn't do.

Did I mention I was new at this thing? And that I rush into new passions with excess enthusiasm?

With much sounder wisdom, I invested in five wrecked cars, carefully chosen. The idea was to fix them up at Dad's shop and sell them for a profit. It was a nice way to turn some of the money into an investment. This left me with $28,000 that went into my bank account.

So I had a lot going on. But there was still wondering when I was going to start preaching. Others would have seen that as a goal to work toward; I saw it as an urgent task to rush into.

Every night I prayed, "Lord, you've called me to preach, but no one's asked me yet. I don't have a pastor for a dad, and I barely know any Christians, so how's this going to happen?"

At that moment, I remembered: *You don't have a sermon ready even if someone asks you to preach. You don't know the first thing about preaching, not to mention the second thing!*

Still, I felt God wanted me to preach. I just needed material.

I turned on the local Christian radio station, Lifesongs, and listened to four different preachers—Alistair Begg, Charles Stanley, Michael Youseff, and John MacArthur. I took notes on their content and style while working at my father's Collision Center during the day. They were so powerful in their delivery, yet I could believe God had equipped me to communicate like this.

I'd done well with Network Marketing, the "Closer's Corner," and as a DJ. It was all about connecting with people. The big difference was that it was no longer entertainment.

The message was about the only things in life that really mattered. I felt I could do this.

I sat down to write a sermon, using the story of Jesus and the two thieves on the cross from Luke 23. It was a story that really touched me. Jesus was crucified between two thieves, one of them cursing him, the other one showing true faith and asking Jesus to remember him in heaven. It was a great way to share the gospel; one of those men was doomed, while the other would live forever in eternity. I could explain the significance of the cross, tell about those two men and their attitudes, and ask, "Which one are you?"

The following week, a man walked up to me at Celebration Church, where I had started attending on Saturday nights, and asked, "Robby, are you a preacher?"

I said, "As a matter of fact, yes, I'm a preacher." It didn't occur to me that it's probably good to have preached at least once before identifying yourself as a preacher, but I was confident I had been called by God.

He told me about the church's downtown mission, the Brantley Baptist Center. "We feed and shelter people on the streets. Volunteers make the whole thing work— meals, maintenance, preaching. Homeless folks come in and receive a meal. In addition to getting fed physically, they get fed spiritually through the Word, so we're always looking for someone to come and bring a message. Would you come next week and preach?"

God had heard my prayer.

I told my parents the next day, "Guess what? I'm going to preach at a church service downtown." They looked at me and wondered one more time if I was on drugs again. They'd been through a few whiplash-turn changes of direction with me, but this one was a bit much. They knew all about priests, but they didn't know one who'd recently been a drug dealer.

I invited them to come hear me, and of course they did, incredibly curious to see what happened when their son stood up to deliver a sermon. My parents had come dressed in the clothing they'd wear to their own church—slacks, button up shirt, and Florsheims for Dad—and there we were, surrounded by seventy-five homeless people.

It was my trial run; I had no idea what I was doing. What I did have was my story—what it was like to be a two-time slave to drug addiction, and how Jesus had rescued me. I told it all.

When I gave an invitation, seven men stood up with tears in their eyes, came forward, and gave their lives to Christ. You could sense the Lord's presence in a palpable way. I was thrilled and thankful. For me it was the confirmation that this was what God wanted me to do with the rest of my life.

I celebrated with those new believers, prayed with them, then caught up with my parents in the parking lot. My dad pulled me off to the side and said, "Son, that was very good. But if I were you, I wouldn't talk publicly about your drug past. I don't think anyone should hear about that."

"Dad, I know it seems strange. But you have to understand that my past isn't something to hide. It's my story. It shows how great God is, to change someone as messed up as me. The story is all I have, and you see how it can touch people." He still seemed doubtful.

I preached again at the Brantley Center. My parents showed up again. This time a man stepped forward afterward to shake my hand. His face was worn and tattered, but he looked vaguely familiar somehow. He said, "Robby, you may not remember me, but I used to be married to Dr. Casey."

Then it all came together. I had once bought all those drugs from Dr. Casey at her all-night clinic. She had a husband who was a police officer and part of her protection. Of course he'd become very wealthy from the scam they had going on. My dad and I had gotten to know him when we fixed up his wrecked BMW, as part of our deal—though Dad had never suspected the real arrangement. To him, it was just another job.

The husband had gotten addicted to drugs himself, as did so many others who got caught up in that world. He'd lost everything, and now here he was, homeless, getting a meal and hearing a sermon at the Brantley Center with other hurting souls. My sermon had meant something to him.

"I appreciate what you've shared tonight," he said. "For the first time in years, I feel hopeful, seeing all that God is doing in you."

And it was then, for the first time, that it all clicked for my parents. They understood that what I was doing was not another one of their son's fads. This was real. This was something that had turned my life around, and it could do that for other people, too. They'd seen it with their own eyes. Here was a shady cop, one they'd met, who had also been to the bottom like me. And now, by the serendipity of God's grace, his path and mine crossed under such different circumstances. Now Mom and Dad understood.

It would be a little while before they came to a saving faith of their own, but God was working in their lives; that was clear. He's always working. It doesn't matter who you are, where you've been, or where you're going. God has a plan, and he's calling you to himself—step by step on a thousand-step journey to him.

Chapter 14

THE BODY NEVER FORGETS

Across the bay from New Orleans, forty miles up the Lake Pontchartrain Causeway, is a tiny Louisiana town called Madisonville. One day in 2003, a telephone rang in a small home there. The call was picked up by Jeremy Brown, my old friend from college who had told me everything I knew about Jesus Christ; Jeremy, who had planted the truth in my mind that no matter what I did, no matter how much trouble I got in, God still loved me and would forgive me.

My old friend picked up the phone and said, "Hello?"

"Jeremy! This is Robby, man! How's it going?"

"Robby? Are you kidding me? Hey, it's great to hear from you! What's up?"

"I just got saved! So listen, Jeremy—God has called me to be a preacher and also to start a ministry with you."

"*What?* Robby—what are you talking about? I haven't heard from you in seven years. Slow down! First of all, you're saying you got saved? And this time, for real?"

"Absolutely! Greatest thing that's ever happened to me. I'm not the same person I used to be. Jeremy, I wrecked my life, man. I was on drugs, but God broke through to me, and he used everything you told me back in college."

"Okay! And second of all, you're saying you've got a call to preach?"

"Already started! I shared my testimony and saw several guys come to the Lord, and—"

"Wait, wait—will you slow down? Man, this is too much at one time. We haven't talked in seven *years*, and you call up, and just like that you want me to take off with you and do some kind of ministry? I know you're crazy, Robby, and I love that about you. But I have a church job here. I'm a youth pastor. God hasn't told me he wants us to be in ministry together."

"Well, seems like I remember, Jesus walked up to folks and said, 'Follow me,' and they put down their fishing nets and walked away with him, right?"

"Yeah, well, that's true, but you ain't Jesus, and I'm not a fisherman. I can't just uproot my life and take off because Robby has another wild idea. Two things. First, you're going to have to tell me more about what's been going on with you. Second, I'm going to have to pray about this thing." We agreed to circle back to the idea later.

I understood how most of the rest of the world looked before they leaped, unlike how I did things. I was willing to be patient this time. Then again, I was on fire and blazing away. Jeremy understood how to follow Jesus, how to grow as a disciple, and I knew he and I had great chemistry. It seemed like a perfect combination for us to work together.

He called me back a week or two later. "Well, I prayed about it," he said. "I was out driving when suddenly I had this urge to pull over by the side of the road and talk to God about this thing. And when I did, the Lord impressed on my heart that I should say yes. I can't believe that happened.

I felt like I needed to warn God about you, but I guess he knows you better than I do. So here's what I'm thinking. This thing can work if we start out ministering at student events. That's where you and I could connect best. Do you still do those magic tricks?"

"Like riding a bike. Muscle memory—the body never forgets."

"Well, students love magic tricks. We saw that ourselves. Could you work a gospel presentation around some tricks?"

"Oh sure! I've been thinking about a few illusions that would work. Since I'm the one that does the tricks, I would need to be the one sharing about Jesus while I did them. You still play guitar and sing, right?"

"Yep. I play for the students in my ministry. I'll lead worship."

"Well, there we have it! How do we find some venues?"

"I know some people that can probably get us booked—youth retreats, ski retreats, church events. We'd have to start small and let word-of-mouth conversations open doors for us."

"I'm ready yesterday."

"Let's keep praying about it, and ask God to really bless this ministry, Robby."

———

That's how Gallaty and Brown Ministries began, and it would become a huge growing experience for me. Apparently, youth pastors loved booking events in which someone drew students in with magic tricks, or "illusions," as some in church circles reminded me. Gallaty and Brown Ministries was on its way up. We had T-shirts, devotional CDs, even a website to create excitement—somewhat of a novelty in 2003. Jeremy would lead the audience in some praise songs, then he'd introduce me. I would capture the crowd's interest quickly with some of my better illusions, then I would read a couple of Bible verses, talk about their meaning, and demonstrate with a trick. We could feel the Lord's hand on what we were doing.

The highlight of our experience had to be the ski trip we attended in West Virginia, with a huge crowd of kids. I was still really new at this thing, and the way I saw it, the best thing to do was to let the Holy Spirit lead me in what to teach. So as we got on the bus, Jeremy asked me, "What are your messages going to be for the retreat?"

"No clue," I smiled.

"What? You're yanking my chain, right?"

"No—not at all. God will give me the messages."

"Robby. You're responsible for five messages. We're being paid to do this, and these kids are counting on being fed spiritually. You *have* to know what you're teaching. God honors preparation. He'd rather you study, wrestle with it, and pray over it than just wing it and leave everything up to him. Do you think I just let God give me music while I'm in front of the audience? Or do I practice and learn good songs?"

"I see what you mean. I never thought of it that way."

Jeremy rolled his eyes. He knew I'd been born again, but I'd brought a whole lot of the old Robby insanity with me. Maybe that could even be a good thing.

I actually preached through Daniel, and somehow the Lord blessed my seat-of-the-pants preparation. Daniel was a young guy who honored God even though he was in a hostile culture—a great case study for students. While everyone skied during the day, I hunkered down in my room developing sermons. What I lacked in depth, I made up for in excitement, and that counts for a lot with that age group.

For the final night, the organizers of the retreat wanted me to give an invitation. I spoke from the Scriptures as usual, but then I shared my story of addiction and deliverance. You could feel God moving in the room. There are times when he shows up in a powerful way, and there's a special, electric intensity in the air. This was one of those evenings. I gave an invitation for the students to give their whole selves to Christ as Jeremy played his guitar. A little into the song, a guy came forward to give his life to the Lord. Then a girl stepped up, tears in her eyes.

I looked over at Jeremy and signaled for him to keep playing. In my spirit was the assurance there were a lot of kids in the room who were right on the edge of a decision. I urged them to listen to God's voice and make a commitment for Christ today, to give him their future.

Someone else came forward. Then another. Jeremy had to keep playing. After thirty minutes, the room was filled with the tears of students. We had a large group of commitments; many were crying out in repentance and giving their lives to Christ for salvation. Jeremy and I were as overcome emotionally as everyone else in the room. We'd never seen God at work like this.

When it was all over, Jeremy showed me his hands, bloody from strumming chords all that time without a pick. His fingers were raw, but his soul was flying high. So was mine.

The ministry was going well, but I had so much to learn as a baby Christian myself. My greatest vulnerability was that

I saw myself as having no vulnerability. With Jesus in my heart, what could go wrong? I'd put my past totally behind me, as I saw things. Looking back, what I really needed was a mentor by my side, someone to keep me accountable and watch my spiritual blind side. Jeremy wasn't there during the weekdays; it was just me on my own, thinking I was ready to save the world.

One day, during the usual, quiet week, I was restless and decided to drive my shiny new Cadillac through some of my old stomping grounds and show them what God could do. That would get them thinking, right?

It was Mardi Gras season. And here was Gallaty, who used to be broke, strung out, and miserable—now clean, sober, and driving the best ride in town. This would open some eyes with the old crowd—then I could tell them about Jesus.

I had the best of intentions, and I was right that every single one of my old friends needed salvation. They were blind to it, just as I'd been.

I turned up the stereo to ear-splitting levels and drove by the house where some of my old buddies lived. I was playing hip-hop, but the rapping was all about Jesus now—DJ Maj, Grits, and KJ-52. A couple of my friends were out. Rocky walked up to my window and said, "Hey, Gallaty, where did you get this car, dude?"

I grabbed his hand. "Jump in and I'll tell you all about it!"

My two friends climbed in, and we headed to the French Quarter. Everybody loved cruising, especially during this time of year. With the windows down and the music amped, everybody would stop what they were doing and watch us go by—three guys rocking a Caddy with Jesus rap booming through the speakers. It felt great to me, as if I was the returning hero, the "after" half of the classic before-and-after story. And I was giving all the glory to God.

Naïve though I may have been, there wasn't anything wrong with any of this—except me. I wasn't ready to withstand temptation. I was the weak link in my own idea.

This was a Friday night. I said, "Tell you what—I'll come back tomorrow and we'll just cruise again. Listen to music and drive through the streets. You guys know I'm not on drugs anymore, so we're not going to get into any trouble."

"Sure, Robby. Let's do it."

The next day I picked up three friends, all still addicts as they'd been before, and we laughed, drove around, and blared our music. After a while, one of them said, "Hey, can we stop at the gas station and get a few beers?"

I wasn't going to drink with them, so it was no big deal, right? I was working on these relationships, showing I wasn't judging them. I knew Jesus met people right where they were and started from there.

Now they were drinking as we drove up and down the streets of the French Quarter. One of them was standing up through the sunroof, talking to people as we went by. Some of the girls were trying to climb into the car. This was the Saturday when the Endymion parade rolled, one of the largest parade days of Mardi Gras, and we were creating a kind of happy mayhem, which had always been my favorite environment.

The next time they asked for a beer stop, I said, "Sure— and, hey, get me one, too." Somewhere in the back of my mind, a red light was flashing, but I ignored it. My problem was drugs, not alcohol, I told myself—though I'd had it explained to me that a buzz is a buzz, and anything could set me off.

I was trying to do a good thing with my old friends. But if you're surrounded by people in a room, and you're standing on a chair, what's easier—to pull your friends up or to be pulled down? The law of gravity answers that one, and I was already feeling that tug. With the beer, I was on my way down from my height; with the cigarette, which always had to go with a beer, I was down a little more. I was smoking and drinking, and boy, I felt good.

At first, some of these guys hadn't trusted me; they thought I might be an informer. But I was building trust.

I thought about a couple of guys I particularly wanted to save—I felt God was really laying them on my heart. One of them was Elliot, with whom I'd come so close to being arrested with drugs in the car on St. Claude. He lived in Jackson Square in a multilevel apartment, and I called him on the phone and asked if I could come by and hang out, tell him what God was doing in my life. He told me to come by any time.

When I got to Elliot's apartment, I said, "Do you mind if I sit down and share about my life?"

"Sure, fine. Do you mind if I roll a joint while you do it?"

I smiled and told him to go ahead. Remember, I was invincible.

After that, things become blurry over a two-week period. I do remember visiting his apartment several times during those weeks, but I can't tell you the exact events leading up to the day the wheels came off.

One Saturday night, less than two weeks from the first joyride in the Cadillac, I was walking back to Elliot's apartment, Bud Light in hand, to snort an eight-ball of coke, while I talked about Jesus with less and less credibility. I'd hit floor level. Somewhere along the line, it became too easy to give in, I let myself get pulled down, and I found out just how un-invincible I was.

———

As I've said, you don't "start over again" with addictions; you pick right up where you left off. This is the main reason so many people die when they relapse. I'd told Jeremy "the body never forgets," but I was talking about illusions. The body never forgets addiction either. The real "illusion" was that I, as a Christian, was invincible, bulletproof, unconquerable.

Was I a new creation in Christ? Saved? Born again? Absolutely.

Was I still a target for temptation? Still capable of stumbling and falling back into slavery? That too. Even Jesus, in the garden, said to Peter, "The spirit is willing, but the flesh is weak."

Me too. I had a spirit hungry for God, *and* a body that still craved all the substitutes that do nothing but destroy.

Because the body never forgets.

Chapter 15

THE PUT-ON

Now I was a Christian, and a Christian addict. How could this happen?

It was, of course, my spiritual ignorance and naiveté, but also my need for accountability. We all need that—impulsive, addictive personalities need it all the more.

I'd once been an addict without a penny. Later, I became one again with a monthly check from the lawyer. Now I was one with a large bank account from the final settlement—$28,000 in the bank and a tremendous need for a high. To this day, I'm not sure why that deadly combination didn't take me right out of this life, like so many of my friends.

Correction: I do know why. The grace, love, and master plan of God are the only possible explanation. Despite all my self-destructive impulses, he continued to watch over me. "I am sure of this, that he who started a good work in you will carry it on to completion until the day of Christ Jesus" (Phil. 1:6).

On the weekends, I was telling students all about Jesus as I performed magic tricks. Jeremy had no idea what was really going on with me. He'd moved forward in faith to do this ministry—faith not only in God, but in his old friend who claimed he was clean and sober. He never suspected that, during the week, as each day went by, I blew through three hundred dollars or more. Sometimes it was a thousand, if I was partying seriously and had some friends along. I no longer bought from Elliot. I could go straight to the Pimp, who respected healthy bank accounts like mine. I was a big-time customer now.

I'd wake up at maybe 10:30 or 11:00 in the morning and go immediately to the New Orleans Original Daiquiris shop to get my early buzz going. The bartender there was named Christy, and over the weeks I got to know her pretty well. I was still under the impression I was an evangelist whose main work was sharing Christ, though I was high most of the time. I talked about Jesus non-stop.

I chatted with Christy as I ordered another 190 Octane Large, a specialty of the house. It had orange juice, so I thought of it as my morning beverage. Christy would polish glasses or unpack bottles, listening with a bemused expression as I talked about all the things Jesus was doing in my life. I wasn't a sloppy drunk, especially this time of day—but it was a strange picture, a guy starting in early every morning while trying to win souls. I was a slave pretending to be free. I knew I'd be going to see the Pimp as soon as I started to feel good. Slowly, $28,000 was changing hands from me to the Pimp—a very expensive lesson in accountability.

$27,500.

$27,000

$26,500 . . .

Each day my bank account dropped another few hundred bucks. I can remember the day I stood at the ATM and looked at the receipt. I'd drained it to the last penny in less than two months. Right back to where I started, all my personal injury money gone into the Pimp's pocket.

THE PUT-ON

Now I had to face facts. My addiction was as powerful as it had ever been, my system cried out for higher highs just to be able to feel anything, and my resources were depleted. I'd gone full circle, back to being a pauper with a habit. I didn't have to ask, "What are you trying to teach me, Lord?" The lesson wasn't complicated at all. Sin is slavery, and Christ could save my soul—but his saving me was a call to walk away from my old life.

I realized that from that day onward, I was looking at life as an addict. Addictive impulses are forever—whether it's drugs, drink, or plain old disobedience to God. The addiction is primarily sin, not drugs, and the old Robby still isn't totally dead.

This is a mystery the Bible teaches us. In one sense, when we are saved, we're totally saved. We're completely free from the punishment we deserve for our sin, and the Bible even says we're free from the power of sin. We don't have to keep sinning. The old self was crucified with Christ, God's Word tells us.

But even though the old self is crucified with Christ, we're told to put the old self to death. So, the old self dies with Christ on the cross, but he keeps trying to get back up day after day, and God calls us to put him to death. That old self will hang around until Jesus returns or calls us home. On that day, we will be free from the power, penalty, and even *presence* of sin; but until then, we're all recovering sin addicts, being called day after day to put the old self to death.

I had to come to terms with the fact that every single day my old self would try to rise up and give in to drugs again. Or try to make life all about Robby and his ego, rather than God and his glory.

That old Robby has to be watched constantly, because he has all kinds of ideas to get the shackles back on my hands and feet. He would love to build a new prison in whatever form.

An old preacher named D. L. Moody once said, "The problem with a living sacrifice is that it keeps crawling off the altar." I'd presented myself as a living sacrifice to Christ, but I didn't understand the "living" part.

How was I able to live these two lives at the same time? I didn't see it as a "put-on" to share the gospel with Christy or preach to kids, all the while getting high. I was in denial.

And the addiction was building again. My nervous system was always calling out for more. I can remember snorting in a hotel room before preaching—not even keeping the two lives separate anymore. I was witnessing while drunk, preaching while high. Jeremy just thought it was Crazy Robby. I never talked to him about it, but together we saw the crowds grow smaller and smaller. Maybe he sensed in his spirit that something wasn't right. The season of Gallaty-Brown Ministries was drawing to a close.

I realized I was no longer listening to God. Once his voice had been like a song in the back of my consciousness, whose Artist I'd finally identified. Then, as a new Christian, that song was pure joy in the forefront of everything I was doing or thinking. Now, the song fell silent. God wasn't speaking to me anymore. I cried out to him—had he deserted me in disgust? That couldn't be. Not the God I knew. Instead, I was confronted with a choice.

"Choose," God was saying. "Choose your path. Will you follow me, or will you stay on that road to self-destruction?" From here on out, I sensed, maybe my life would no longer be spared. Maybe one day, my parents would have a door broken down and once again make their way into an empty, cold apartment; they'd find my wasted body, alone and sur-rounded by the substances that finally took my life away.

———

One of our final bookings was at Kosciusko, Mississippi. There were four hundred students in attendance. I came out, said a couple of words to the audience, and began with a classic trick, involving a nervous volunteer from the audience.

> Pick a card, any card. When you've seen what it is, place it back in the deck. Notice I don't touch it or see it. Okay? Now, I want you to write the suit and the number on a Post-It note. Got it? Now fold up the note, and place it here in the ashtray. Can you light it on fire? Here's a lighter. Everyone notice: it has burned to ashes.

I reached into the ashtray with my right hand and held it up to show the audience the ashes all over my hand. I then rubbed my hand over my left forearm—where the King of Hearts appeared burned into my arm.

With a little preparation, it's a great trick that nearly always wows the audience. *Nearly* always. But this time, at the triumphant moment, I showed my forearm and a girl in the crowd shouted, "That's of the devil!"

This had never happened before. I looked around at the nervous faces of the kids, many of them moving from smiles to questioning. I thought, *The invitation won't go well tonight.*

And it didn't. I couldn't help but think about the ski retreat in West Virginia, and what that room felt like—the presence of the Spirit so heavy it was overwhelming.

Tonight was nothing like that. I thought of a verse in the Old Testament, "The glory of the Lord has departed."

It's of the devil.

We got fewer bookings. When we did have one, the numbers were small. I felt ineffective. I stopped hearing from Jeremy—not until a year later, when he called to invite me to preach at his church, did we speak again.

I felt all alone again. I was also broke, the settlement money all gone. Hard heads need hard lessons, but I also know that if it had cost a million bucks, the price would have been cheap. I could stand to be broke; what I couldn't handle was the wall that had risen between God and me.

On one of my routine morning daiquiri runs, Christy the bartender came to faith in Christ for the first time. After a month of sharing the gospel every morning, she finally prayed to receive Christ. I remember her handing me a Large 190 Octane daiquiri, the strongest they make, and saying to me, "For someone who knows so much about Jesus, you sure don't act like it." To her, my act must have seemed like a put-on.

Her words stopped me in my tracks.

In the process of using me to lead her to the Lord, God used her to bring me back to him.

Now I decided I was ready to walk away from drugs for the third time, but this time it had to be for good. Forever. I might stumble, I might make mistakes, but not *this* particular stumble. Not in this area of my life. Drugs and drunkenness were over. I chose Jesus, and my body was going to be a proper temple from here on out.

This time there would be no clinics. No rehab. I would depend totally on the power of God. I had a ceremonial ritual by my bedside, showing myself that I was sacrificing all my paraphernalia once and for all. I cried out once more to

THE PUT-ON

God, "Don't take your presence from me!" Only by his sovereign grace could I succeed in being the person he wanted me to be. It was by his power and love that I made a personal covenant to no longer put myself in position for the devil to take me down. I prayed for a long time, wept, and repented to the depth of my soul.

This was a direct, miraculous transformation—not something that occurs for everyone. Since then, I've worked with thousands of people dealing with addictions, and I know this kind of deliverance is rare. Most of the time, someone struggling shouldn't hesitate to seek professional help from doctors or a special clinic. God works through those means as well, just as he works through insulin if you're a diabetic.

My situation was unique. All I know is that, when I rose from the bed, I was again a changed man. Jesus had calmed the storm, so that my system was quiet once more, and the presence of God had returned. From that day to this one, for more than a decade and a half, I've been sober. More important even than sober, I've been honest about my utter weakness. No more illusions of being bulletproof. Like Paul the apostle, who speaks to me so powerfully through the Scriptures, I know I'm the "chief of sinners," and I have no option but to live in daily dependence upon him. Not annual. Not weekly. *Daily.*

Yes, Jesus saved me once and for always. Once that occurred, on November 11, 2002, it was a done deal. My eternal fate was sealed. But there's eternal salvation, and then there's the physical world, where I have to live. Every day, as long as I make my residence here, I have to get out of bed and put on Christ even as I put on the day's clothing. The Bible commands me to "put on Christ like a garment" (Gal. 3:27 HCSB). In another verse, I'm told to "put on the new self, the one created according to God's likeness"

(Eph. 4:24). Later in Ephesians, I'm told to put on battle armor. Every day is spiritual conflict. The good news is that in God's power, every single battle is winnable. And the war itself, ultimately, has already been won on the cross.

No one explained things like that to me when I first became a Christian, but I get it now. There's a reason Paul used that word picture over and over, the idea of getting dressed. I have to start early in the day and take in his grace rather than the impulses of my flesh. If I want to live in his freedom and be liberated from servitude to sin, that's what my life has to look like.

For several dangerous months, I lived two lives. Mercy was extended to me. I'm eternally grateful for his grace. Today and every day, from here onward, I plan to put on Christ and fight the good fight.

Chapter 16

HERE I AM, SEND SOMEBODY

L ife had become very quiet, a rarity for me. I'd gotten off drugs for the final time, with a new understanding of temptation's power and my weakness.

Before the preaching opportunities dried up completely, God opened the door for one last message on Easter Sunday. I was invited to preach at a little church called Creedmoor Presbyterian, just down the road from Chalmette in Toca, Louisiana. There were usually about twelve people in attendance, but when my whole family showed up to support me, it almost doubled the average crowd.

There was something different about standing in a traditional pulpit to preach instead of talking to students and using magic tricks. I spoke way too rapidly, stumbled over my words a few times, and realized I was no master of the pulpit. Still, it was exciting to be preaching in a church on Easter Sunday—especially when the doors swung quietly open midway through the sermon, and here came three of the four girls from William Carey—Julie, who had introduced me to T-Bone, Rebecca, who lived in Baton Rouge, and another. Julie had kept the other girls informed on my activities and had brought them along for emotional support.

They drove two hours to hear me preach. I could feel their encouragement from across the room.

As I preached, I realized the girls started to cry. The more I preached, the more the girls cried. I thought, *Maybe this preaching thing isn't working out for me.*

After the service, there were hugs and tears all around. I asked Rebecca, "Why are you girls crying?"

"Robby, you didn't know it, but we were praying for you all through college. We prayed you'd get saved. We just had a feeling about it, thinking about all the ways you could serve God if he ever got hold of your life. Four of us made a commitment to pray for you every day, and now, seven years later, when Julie told us you were preaching—we just had to come and see it for ourselves. God has shown us a miracle this morning."

I tell people now to keep praying for the person you know who is the farthest from God—you never know just how God is going to answer that request.

———

Later, the deacons asked me to consider becoming the pastor at their church. I wasn't ready to be a pastor. I learned at this point I needed to be discipled before I could make disciples. But I'll always remember Creedmoor Presbyterian Church. It's not there any longer—just a forlorn patch of trees and rubble on Bayou Road. Hurricane Katrina leveled it, along with the town of Toca, where it was located.

It's easy to look back, recall that first Sunday morning sermon, see again those girls coming through the church door, and realize God was trying to break through to me.

After that, opportunities to preach pretty much dried up. I was broken but at peace, a young Christian wandering his way along in the faith. My ministry venture with Jeremy had played out. The cash settlement was all gone. I prayed, took stock of my life, and decided I needed someone to come alongside me. I felt the need to connect with people like me—those who were done with partying and ready to become serious about spiritual issues.

I got together with a few friends from my old life, Brian and Brandon, who were now believers, and we began to meet for prayer and Bible study together. My grandfather was living with my parents at this time, so he allowed us to pray in his otherwise empty house every day. While our group sought God together, we also celebrated our sobriety and found ways to serve God. On Friday nights, after an hour on our faces in prayer, we'd hop into my Cadillac and go looking for unsuspecting lost people, in order to share our faith with them.

Naturally, we cruised by our old stomping grounds. These were our people, young adults like us who were still seeking meaning and purpose through pleasure and sensuality. We felt a genuine burden to see them discover the love of God the way we had.

Maybe we were a little reckless. I remember an occasion when we spotted a couple of guys walking down the street, probably from one bar to the next. There were four of us in the car. We cruised by the two guys, made a sharp U-turn, and screeched to a halt in a parking lot just behind them. We threw open the four doors of the black Cadillac like a *Cops* episode.

The two guys freaked out and took off, running for their lives. "We come in the name of Jesus!" we bellowed as we set off in hot pursuit.

We caught one of the guys, got him calmed down, and started telling him about Jesus rather than reading him his Miranda rights. He looked from one of us to the other, figuring maybe he was out of his mind. Then he started to chuckle. Then he started to listen and to respond. We showed him his need for Christ, and he prayed with us.

Somewhere in the midst of all this, his friend wandered up nervously. Hearing what we were talking about, he said, "I've heard about Jesus. But this is the first time I've ever seen him pull up in a Cadillac."

This was our Friday night routine for several months. In a way, it was just as crazy as the Fridays when we were partying, just a whole lot less common in New Orleans. A lot of amazing conversations came out of that period. We were a street Christian militia, attacking from the front lines.

I was a fairly new believer who told everyone about Jesus. New believers tend to be the ones with the most enthusiasm, the ones most likely to lead others to Christ. They're unashamed and unrestrained in their enthusiasm. Nobody has told them to keep their faith politely hidden. It's a shame that as time goes on, we too often learn to hide from the needs of the world in our churches and fellowship groups. Sadly, many have gotten over being saved. We forget that at one time we were lost and needed salvation. We have become so institutionalized and domesticated that we overlook and look over the people Jesus came to save.

Even though I was zealous to share my faith, I had learned from past mistakes never to go out alone or venture into my old environments. No one is immune from falling. What takes years to build in the form of a testimony can be lost in a minute to sin.

I was still longing to grow as a believer. I was now learning enough to know how much I needed to learn—just wise enough to know I lacked wisdom. I was going to church and that helped. I had people to pray with, a community to grow with. But I needed that committed mentor. My friend Julie compared me to a sponge. "You're just soaking in every drop, but you need somebody to disciple you. Your growth needs to be solid and intentional. You're a Timothy who needs a Paul," she said.

"I guess," I said, with a vague understanding of who Timothy was. "But where do you go to get a Paul?"

"You pray for it," she said. "Just tell God what you need, and keep asking. No matter how impatient you get, keep right on asking—that's the main thing, not the words or the form. He *will* answer you. Why *wouldn't* he answer that kind of prayer?"

So while Isaiah's prayer was "Here am I, send me," mine was more like, "Here am I—send somebody!" I figured he would have to be a special kind of believer, loaded down not only with wisdom but heroic patience. But surely he was out there.

One Sunday I was at church, praying as the service ended, when a guy walked up to me. He looked like he was about fifteen years old—like the kind of kid who'd love my magic tricks. It turned out he was only two years younger than me. His name was David Platt.

"Hey, man," he said, offering his hand. "I've seen you praying around here. I heard you were looking for someone to meet with you to grow as a believer. I was wondering if you would be interested in hanging out once a week to talk about the Scriptures, memorize the Word, and pray."

I responded enthusiastically.

"Why don't you pray about it?"

"Already did that. When do we meet?"

I could tell he was a very intense guy, and he was surprised by the degree to which I was ready to hit the ground running. We began to talk about times and places, and this began a weekly tradition of meeting for pizza or General Tso's chicken, and talking over the Scriptures and life.

My story was an eye-opener for David. He was a product of the Atlanta suburbs. He'd been raised as a Baptist and been taught the gospel. He didn't have a fiery conversion experience like I had. He'd gone to high school, then college, then seminary, without playing college basketball, performing as a magician, learning Brazilian Jiujitsu, working as a bartender-comedian, or becoming a hard-core drug addict. As a student at the University of Georgia, David was already preaching all over the country. The most exciting highlight of his life probably happened in the seminary library, where he was working on his PhD. This made us somewhat of an odd couple.

"You're telling me the truth?" he asked as I gave him the short version of my own journey. (I get that a lot.) David was studying here in town at New Orleans Baptist Theological Seminary. While I'd been living out an un-filmed Reality TV life, he'd been learning a powerful command of Scripture. While I understood the power of sin from personal experience, he understood everything the Bible had to say about it. So we had some incredible back-and-forth conversations. This was a transformational relationship in my life. Julie had been right. God answered my prayer in a fantastic way.

————

In the fifteen years that followed, David became pastor of a megachurch at the age of twenty-six, he became president of the International Mission Board of the Southern Baptist Convention, helping to transform that organization, and he wrote an international bestseller, *Radical*, which created a whole movement and started a national conversation.

Now he's back in the pastorate, in Virginia. After all this activity, he's moved from looking fifteen to about twenty. I joke with him about his baby face, but his faith was anything but childlike.

Each week, I'd drive by the seminary and pick David up. We'd have lunch, then I'd drop him off for his next class. Over the meal, I'd take in every word he spoke and realize I needed to preserve it. I'd start scribbling furiously on a napkin. Soon I'd have to ask the waiter for another napkin. Finally David watched me jotting, tearing a hole in the thin paper with my pen, and said, "You know, they make these things called notebooks. They're not hard to find. I find them to be superior to napkins."

"Good point. Let me write it down." I summoned the waiter for another one.

"You'll lose the napkin, right? But you're wise to take notes. Once you leave here, you'll forget most of what you've heard, no matter how closely you pay attention."

I nodded. I knew he was right. This wasn't like history class back in high school—everything David taught me seemed to relate to how I lived every day.

He continued, "Try to remember, you're not learning for you."

"I'm not?"

"You're learning for the next guy, the one who comes behind you."

I looked over my shoulder at the busy restaurant, then turned back to David. "The thing is, nobody's coming behind me," I said. I felt like a period instead of a comma at this point in my journey. Who wanted to hear what I had to say?

"Maybe right now there's nobody, Robby. But someday there will be. The message came to you because it was on its way to somebody else. It always is. The people who shared it with you—they got it for the same reason. It's like a relay race. Everybody's either handing off the baton or fumbling it."

I learned at that point that the dullest pencil is better than the sharpest mind.

I was always anxious to write things down, but another part of me wanted to sit and reflect on what he was saying. David saw the big picture, which was new to me. He had an eternal perspective of everyday things, and for me, that was mind-boggling.

He took a sip of his tea and said, "Robby, I want you to pray about something. I want you to explore whether God wants you to go to seminary, here at New Orleans. God has gifted you to preach and teach his Word, so you should pray about a degree in preaching."

This time I looked long and hard before leaping. A seminary degree was about the last thing that would have occurred to me. "David, I don't even know good English," I said.

"You'll be fine. Moses made that kind of argument when God called him. 'I can't do it. I'm not good enough.' And God always has the same response. If he wants you to do this, he will equip you for the task. Think of it this way: the next four to eight years of your life will equip you for the next forty years of ministry."

David was an encourager. He always believed I could do things I doubted I could do. He was Paul to my Timothy.

In only our second meeting, David announced we were going to memorize Scripture.

"Okay," I said. "I can probably handle that. Which verse?"

He laughed. "Verse? Verses. Passages. Whole chapters!"

"Wait—no," I stammered. "You don't understand, man. I can't do that."

I proceeded to give David a five-minute education on the effects of drugs and alcohol on the brain. "If you do all the drugs I did, for as long as I did, your mind is like a big basket with a hole in it. Stuff just leaks out the bottom. I can hold a little info, but not a load of it. No way I can memorize long sections of the Bible."

David listened patiently as he ate his lunch. He allowed me to finish, then said, "That's fine. We'll just do four verses a week. You can handle four verses, right?"

"If you say so."

I felt like a guy with a broken leg being told he could slam dunk, but I really wanted to go along with anything my new friend asked me to do. Not only that, but I loved the idea of whole passages of the Bible making their home inside my head. I just figured it wasn't possible.

We started with Romans 1, the opening chapter of Paul's masterwork on faith and salvation. For me, even memorizing a few verses was like trying to master advanced quantum physics—even in small pieces, it was daunting. I spent hours reading and rereading the verses. Then I'd write them down, repeating the phrases out loud. After that, I'd speak the words onto my Sony tape recorder, then lie back with my eyes closed and listen, playing the tapes over and over, trying to match my voice in reciting the phrases.

Little by little, I found I could recite the first chapter of Romans. And we kept right on going. We moved to Romans 2 and then Romans 8. We came to a verse about there being "no condemnation for those who are in Christ Jesus." I needed that one. This may have been the hardest work I'd ever done—but it was the most satisfying. I knew having those majestic words of the apostle in my head would renew an abused, ramshackle brain better than anything in the world.

All this time, I also had an abiding passion to share the gospel with my parents. Of course they were still churchgoing Catholics, and they were glad that at least my new obsession wasn't likely to kill me, as the last one was. In other words, Jesus was a safer drug. They'd heard me speak to homeless people and to a tiny handful of bayou Presbyterians last Easter. They knew I was all in with my faith.

But that was the thing—I'd been all in with plenty of other pursuits. It could be magic or medication, jiujitsu or Jesus, one passion was the same as another. To my parents, it was just another age, another stage.

Not only that, but I wasn't exactly tactful in the way I shared my faith with them. I confronted them on their Catholic teaching, weaponizing my theology. "Why do you think Mary, the mother of Jesus, is a co-Redemptrix with Christ?" I would ask. "Show me one verse in Scripture that backs up that claim."

Or, "Jesus said to call no man Father, so why do you call your priest Father Bob?"

Or, "Where do you find Purgatory in the Bible? Let me read you a couple of verses that say Jesus gives us full access to salvation immediately after death."

You can imagine how well the confrontation method went over. They would just sigh and try to change the subject, or they'd ask me to leave, if it came to that.

You can't badger people into the kingdom of God.

But by Easter of 2004, maybe I was beginning to grow up just a little bit in my faith. I decided to stop the debates. They weren't working. If anything, they were damaging our relationship. The Holy Spirit never seemed present when I was confrontational. So I decided to try something different.

My family was all together for Easter—Mom, Dad, my sister, my uncle, my aunt, and grandpa. I asked for everyone's attention and, without explanation or introduction, I began to recite the opening to the Epistle to the Romans:

> Paul, a slave of Christ Jesus, called as an apostle and singled out for God's good news—which He promised long ago through His prophets in the Holy Scriptures . . . (HSCB)

I don't think anybody in the room understood what I was doing, or that what they were hearing was a straight Bible passage. I watched their eyes as I spoke from pure memory, and I saw a lot of knitted brows and lack of comprehension. As I went on, however, they began to realize where these majestic words came from.

But they'd never heard a passage of the Bible spoken this way. Ever.

I'd lived with those words for months and months; doted on them. I'd planted them in my mind, watered them, tended them, and watched over them to make sure they were taking root. I knew those words intimately, as I knew the features of my own face or the houses in my neighborhood.

The words of Paul's letter to the Romans flowed out of my mouth easily, with the right accents at the right places, because they were much more than words to me by this time. David and I had explored them, inspected them, turned them inside out together. I spoke the mind of Paul and the inspiration of God with meaning and feeling.

I kept on going, since no one stopped me. I moved through the chapters, and the faces shifted from confused to impressed to, finally, deeply moved. In some way, time itself seemed to stop and listen. By the time I reached the soaring finale to Romans 8, the room was completely silent, fully absorbed. My mom and sister had tears rolling down their cheeks at this point.

> There is therefore now no condemnation for those who are in Christ Jesus. For the law of the Spirit of life has set you free in Christ Jesus from the law of sin and death . . .
>
> No, in all these things we are more than conquerors through him who loved us. For I am sure that neither death nor life, nor angels nor rulers, nor things present nor things to come, nor powers, nor height nor depth, nor anything else in all creation, will be able to separate us from the love of God in Christ Jesus our Lord! (vv. 1–2, 38–39 ESV)

I finally finished speaking, and rested with a smile, appreciative of the attention I'd received. My family remained silent for a moment. I knew that somehow, that simple act of recitation had changed something between my family and me. For the first time, I believe they understood that Jesus was more than the next fad in line. He was my life.

They knew that all those other pursuits were empty attempts in the single quest to find what I now had: a living relationship that filled my being and made me complete, in the same way these words from Romans had filled me in their presence.

I could finally answer Paula's question. I knew who I was. Robby Gallaty had an identity.

And now, my parents saw it too.

What I came to understand on that Easter Sunday was that the Word of God truly is far sharper and more powerful than any two-edged sword. Debating and salesmanship come up empty. Logic and persuasion accomplish nothing. But the Word of God needs only to be released. When you have a lion, you don't boast about what it *would* do. You set it loose. You let it roar.

That day, the Word of God was turned loose, and it roared in our household. No one got saved that day. But seeds were planted for a future harvest.

Chapter 17

IGNORANCE
ON FIRE

As the new year began in 2004, I became a student at New Orleans Baptist Theological Seminary (NOBTS). I'd lived all my life in and around this city, but I was hardly aware of NOBTS. It was quiet and Baptist; the city was festive and Catholic.

David Platt had sent me there, or at least toward praying in that direction. That was okay by me, because there was no way they'd accept me, right? I figured I still had Bourbon Street written all over me. Not to mention that I was less than a year removed from drugs and alcohol.

Dr. Chuck Kelley, the school president, eventually heard my eye-opening personal testimony. I asked him after graduation, "Dr. Kelley, I've always wondered. How is it you let a guy like me into a place like this?"

He laughed and said, "Based on your transcript, you were just another William Carey guy—good Baptist school. You didn't exactly fill us in on what you'd been up to ever since."

"You never asked," I said.

He laughed.

The church needs a few students with degrees from the sin world. Sin is an important topic for us. The Bible has its share of sin experts, and the church is supposed to be a hospital for sinners. I knew going in that I'd be an outlier, given the life I'd led. I expected to walk through the seminary corridors and see clusters of students discussing the finer points of Pauline theology, or maybe debating End Times theories. Going to seminary would be just one step below hanging out with the Apostles themselves—these folks might not have visible halos, but they'd be front-row saints.

David Platt was my model of what to expect. But I didn't see a lot of his vision and passion for the gospel on my first few days. It was more like a law school or med school, a typical post-graduate institution. "Hey, David," I asked, "where does the early morning prayer group meet?"

"Prayer group? There isn't one."

I persisted. "Where are the guys on fire for Jesus?"

"Robby, you've got to remember, these are people who mostly grew up as devout believers, the same way I did. Their faith isn't brand-new to them like it is for you. They have more Bible knowledge; you have more passion. You don't know much, but you're utterly *psyched* about the parts you do know."

My nickname in those days was "Ignorance on Fire."

"I guess," I replied. "But when I see a guy falling asleep in class, I want to get in his face and say, 'Wake up, dude! You've got the gospel—the greatest news in history—right there in front of you! How can you be dozing off?'"

"Can't say I disagree. But I think most seminaries and Bible colleges are like this. Most churches, for that matter. By the way, do you want to start meeting for prayer and discipleship before school starts?"

I was in. David and I agreed to Tuesdays and Thursdays at 7:00 a.m. We wanted to see gospel passion spread throughout this campus.

Since David was the assistant to the Dean of the Chapel, he was given a key to Leavell Chapel. For two weeks, just the two of us met for Bible study and accountability on Tuesdays and an hour of prayer on Thursdays. We simply knelt on those stairs, crying out to God to revive us, revive our fellow students, revive our city. Only years later did I understand how special those first few weeks were.

Shortly thereafter, a small but faithful group of guys joined us for Bible study and prayer every week. We focused on our campus, the students' relationships with Christ, and our impact on the world. Twelve to fourteen of us met twice a week, and we didn't sit around, sip coffee, and shoot the bull. We were studying God's Word and on our faces praying.

One day I was walking to that chapel, which was just a block or so from Highway 90 and, just beyond it, I-10. I looked up at the steeple and realized I was standing within shouting distance of the place where my Mustang had been wrecked, four and a half years earlier.

It seemed more like a lifetime. My path had taken a few sharp turns since then. There I stood by a wreck, facing a steeple, with a highway in-between. There was powerful symbolism in that memory. As I gathered with friends beneath that cross, I began to learn what real prayer was all about. What I learned in my classes was valuable; what I learned in the school of prayer was priceless.

———

That spring I began to think about what I was going to do for the summer. This is always a big question for seminary students. The idea is to go into the "field" and get some solid experience, usually in a church setting or at camp. Alternatively, you could stay on campus and study, but most students choose to take summer positions.

I was offered an opportunity that sounded like a blast. The Southern Baptist Convention offers CentriKid Camps for third to sixth graders. They take place all over the nation, and I had a chance to travel and preach five times a week along the East Coast. It would offer me valuable experience ministering to children, lots of preaching time, and of course, the pleasure of travel.

But then another possibility materialized. A campus minister named Tim LaFleur, from Nicholls State in Thibodaux, was looking for a preaching student from the seminary to go with him to New Mexico for the summer. There was a huge camp and conference center there at the foot of the Rocky Mountains. All through the summer, there are programs and special weeks of all kinds—opportunities to work with people from churches across the West.

I was also making plans to guest-preach at Jeremy Brown's church in Madisonville, about an hour and a half from Baton Rouge. My friend Rebecca from college—one of those girls who had prayed for me—called me out of the blue. She told me she knew I wouldn't be too far away from Baton Rouge, and she had a friend she wanted to introduce. She'd be bringing her to come hear me in Madisonville on March 15.

This, of course, sounded an awful lot like a blind date for a preaching event. I wasn't so sure how something like that would work out—how exactly do preaching and dating mix? Maybe that was the Catholic in me . . .

There was so much going on in my life at this point that I wasn't much interested in dating. I was finally experiencing the growth and the biblical understanding I had craved.

I would find out later that Kandi—Rebecca's friend—wasn't too excited about this thing either. She was willing to go along with it, but it probably seemed weird to listen to the proclamation of God's Word while sizing up a preacher as boyfriend material. Blind dates are awkward anyway, about a hundred percent of the time.

A few minutes before the service, I walked to the front of the worship center and greeted the girls. We talked for a few minutes, and I had to admit I was impressed with Kandi—how she carried herself, how her smile set me at ease, how intelligent she clearly was. She was unlike any Christian woman I'd ever met. She had everything any guy could ever pray for, and more.

Kandi had a different perspective of me. She was under the impression I was there as part of the Power Team, there to tear phone books, and not to preach the Word. For months, I'd been back in the gym; I walked in at six-foot-six, 285 pounds.

By the end of the night, I felt that talking to Kandi was like being with someone I'd known for years. Later I found out that she felt the same way about me. The awkwardness vanished for both of us, just like that.

I said to the group, "Would you guys like to come to a room in the back and pray for me before I preach?"

They agreed, and a small group of Rebecca, Kandi, my friend Brian, whom I referred to as Big Bill, and I, did just that. We prayed together that God would use my time in the pulpit to change people's hearts. Kandi still enjoys pointing out that she had the opportunity to pray for me on our very first date, and on every day since. And I enjoy pointing out that, within a two-day period, I met the two people most influential in my life: Kandi, whom I would marry, and Tim LaFleur, who would mentor me.

Back at seminary, Tim invited me to preach at BCM (Baptist Collegiate Ministries) the following night. It would be an interview of sorts, to help him decide whether to offer me the summer position in New Mexico. I preached the same sermon I'd just delivered the night before, "A Recipe for Revival," based on this Old Testament passage:

"If My people who are called by My name will humble themselves, and pray and seek My face, and turn from their wicked ways, then I will hear from heaven, and will forgive their sin and heal their land." (2 Chron. 7:14 NKJV)

It's one of the most well-preached passages about revival. It shows the deep desire God had for his people Israel—a whole nation—to come to repentance. The same promise is true for his people now—Christians. It gives us four powerful steps we can take if we want to claim God's promise of revival. No wonder pastors love preaching this verse.

Tim—or Bro T, as the college kids knew him—listened to me preach the day after I met Kandi. It was a Tuesday worship service at BCM. The following week, he told me he'd like me to be his protégé for a summer of ministry in New Mexico. I'd be investing my time in 130 college students—an amazing opportunity. I think Tim may have seen in me a rough lump of clay that God was ready to mold into a useful vessel.

It sounded great, and I immediately liked Tim. But I still had an open invitation from CentriKid—I'd gotten myself excited about that one, too. Crunching the numbers, I knew I could preach five times a week for CentriKid, but only once in New Mexico. I went back and forth between the two choices. I prayed but received no clear direction.

I happened to grab lunch with my friend and fellow seminary student Byron Townsend after church at Edgewater Baptist the next Sunday. Byron had been discipled by Tim at Nicholls State, and he said a few simple words that changed my life. "Robby," he said, "I know you think you'd get five times as much preaching experience with the younger kids. But spending a summer with Tim LaFleur will change your life. I'm not exaggerating. You'll come back a different guy."

The counsel of a friend, as Proverbs tells us, can be powerful. I marinated in Byron's words for the next two days, and the whole issue became crystal clear. I told Tim I would accept his offer to be camp pastor for the High Point program in New Mexico. I'm not sure I ever made a better decision, other than the day I gave myself to Christ, or the day I said, "I do," to Kandi, ten months later. Those moves would be hard to top.

Like Kandi, I felt like I was with an old friend the first day we spent together. Alongside our official duties, Tim and I began meeting once a week for intentional discipleship. I performed my first baptism in the creek at the camp under his guidance. He showed me how to organize a Bible study, how to properly prepare a sermon, how to grill steaks to perfection, how to cook 200 hamburgers on a stone grill, how to over season them with Tony's Chachere's, and even how to play a mean game of Spades (gambling excluded).

Probably the most valuable lesson had to do with relationships. I watched how he interacted with his wife at just the time I had begun dating Kandi (from March to June, we were together every weekend). Then I saw how he dealt with students who were grappling with their future, with what and whom they wanted to become.

Tim's life-on-life approach was phenomenal. I'd never seen someone so caring, so hands-on, and so adept at changing someone's life in one hour of conversation. It instilled in me a drive to be the kind of catalyst for life-change that he was.

We had incredible late-night conversations, free-wheeling chats about everything from the Second Coming to our assurance of salvation. I was a sponge soaking up every tiny drop. He made little throwaway comments such as, "You can't expect from others what you aren't living out in your own life," and, "The Christian life is easy or impossible—impossible in your own strength, easy if you allow Christ to work in and through you." "If you aim at nothing," he said, "you will hit it every time," and "Ministry is received and not achieved." Years later, we started calling them "Tim-isms."

He'd just toss them out there, and I'd grab them and try fitting them into my brain, which was like a suitcase after a long vacation, where you buy far too many souvenirs to pack. I was loaded down with new ideas and perspectives.

I began to notice a theme in some of these phrases. *Impossible in your own strength . . . received, not achieved.* Finally I told him in one of our discipleship group times, "Tim, you just blew up my whole philosophy of life."

"What do you mean?"

"I used to go around saying, 'If it's meant to be, it's up to me.' My phrase and your phrases don't fit together." I told him about my business networking experience, and what I thought I'd learned about personal success—that it was all about outworking the competition.

Tim said, "Robby, you can't do anything in your own strength—not anything eternally significant. Not anything that gives God glory. The best you can come up with is a righteousness that is like filthy rags before God."

"So my actions are meaningless?"

"Of course not. Hard work is a good thing, but everything should be done in his strength. Jesus says, 'My yoke is easy and my burden is light.' Think of it this way: you have to allow Christ to work *in* you and to work *through* you for his glory."

I heard about a pastor who told the story of enjoying a late afternoon swim in the ocean, down on the Gulf. He lost track of the time, looked back at the shore, and realized he'd gotten way too far away from dry land. He started to panic, realizing he lacked the endurance to swim all the way back to the beach. As his anxiety spiked, he began to struggle. Then he thought about it and realized that the waves always move toward the sand. If he simply relaxed, looked up to the sun and floated on the tide, he would be carried back toward safety.

Tim helped me understand the difference between trying frantically to move in my own strength, which is exhausting, and relaxing into the arms of a loving God, whose strength is infinite, and who wants to guide us toward our best destination. This was an incredible eye-opener for me. That idea alone led me to return from that summer a changed man.

Tim modeled early morning quiet time. He modeled group prayer. He modeled evangelism, Scripture memory—basically all the disciplines of faith. Yet he was probably the most fun person I've ever been around. I began to think, *This is the model of how it works. This is who I want to be. He rides the waves of God's will, and God moves him along effortlessly, yet look at what he accomplishes!*

One thing I forgot to mention about Bro T. He is legally blind. A heart attack years ago affected his sight, leaving him blinded in the hospital. It hasn't slowed him down one bit. "What I lost in sight," Tim says often, "God made up for

PTO

with my memory." Bro T is a walking Bible. He may have the entire New Testament committed to memory.

One week, the camp was hosting a music camp. People came from all over the country to participate. I walked into the dining hall for lunch, and it was filled with faces I didn't know. Except for one. I looked over at a nearby table and spotted Pastor Celoria. Seven years earlier, I'd been trying to build a multilevel marketing business. This man had told me he was placing all his trust in me, and he invested a great sum in our plan based on his people's contributions—and then the business had gone belly-up.

At the time, he was the one client I couldn't face. Who knows how he found out he'd lost it all? It wasn't from me. I'd changed my number, moved on quickly, and carried the burden of that sin ever since. As a nonbeliever, I'd felt it weighing on my conscience. As a Christian, I felt the conviction of the Spirit.

I froze in place when I saw the pastor and his wife all these years later, happily chatting over their lunch. I walked out of the dining hall as quickly as I could. I just didn't have the courage to speak to him. All day I thought about it, and as soon as I had an extra moment with Tim, I told him the story. He listened carefully, nodding along. I finished explaining, and said, "Brother Tim, what should I do?"

He didn't hesitate. "That's an easy one. You have to go and ask for forgiveness. You needed to do it seven years ago, but God has given you a second chance."

"I was afraid you'd say that." I sat and thought about it, prayed about it. Tim was right—I had to face up to it and do the right thing.

I had trouble sleeping that night, but lunchtime came around the next day and I clutched my tray with white knuckles. I found Pastor Celoria and headed his way. He spotted me when I was halfway there, and his face lit up as he recognized me.

"Hi, Brother Celoria," I said.

"Robby! What in the world are you doing here? I haven't seen you in so long. How have you been?"

"Just fine, sir, but I need to say something do you."

"Okay?"

"I owe you an apology," I said. He must have seen my nervousness, and it must have made quite a contrast with the self-assured young guy he'd known. "I treated you poorly. You see, I got the word that our business ran out of money, and I just couldn't—"

When he saw the tears rolling down my cheeks, he stood up and put a hand on my shoulder. "Stop, son, you don't need to apologize for anything. You've just made my day. Will you join us, and tell us why you're here this week? We want to hear what God is doing in your life."

I couldn't believe it. He was honestly delighted to see me! How would I have handled it if I'd been in his shoes? I learned a lesson in forgiveness and mercy I've never forgotten. We had an amazing conversation in which he brought me up-to-date on his church, and I held him spellbound with my testimony. Tears were streaming down his cheeks. His wife wept. So did I. There were hugs all around.

At one point, Brother Celoria looked me in the eye and said to me, "I always knew, Robby, that if God got ahold of your heart, there'd be no telling what he would do with you."

Not only did I learn about forgiveness that day, but also about how God wants to heal our emotional scars—even old ones. If we'll put him first and walk in obedience to him, he'll work in the supernatural realm to bring healing to things we've messed up in the physical realm.

When I came rushing back to Tim to tell him the whole story, he was as happy about it as I was. He was teaching me so many things, but this was a lesson that had to come directly from heaven.

————

During one of my long talks with Tim, I found myself invoking the name "Kandi" for about the ninth time in the last five minutes. I have no idea what the spiritual topic was, but Tim bypassed it. Instead, he said, "Listen, brother, when are you going to marry that girl?"

I gulped. "Tim, I can barely afford to take care of me; I don't have any money. We've just been dating three months or so anyway. I've got three years to go in seminary. I'm a struggling itinerant preacher, and a full-time student who works part-time for his father. I don't know if I'm ready."

"You're ready."

"*What?*"

"Robby, don't you think that if God can care for one, he can care for two? Has he given you a tight budget, or has he asked you to trust him to provide?"

When Tim spoke, I listened. When the summer ended, I came back to Louisiana, bought a ring, and proposed two weeks later. After ten months of dating, we were married on December 18, 2004, one week before Christmas.

I had to stop and catch my breath when I thought about how quickly God was bringing things together in my life—there was no doubt his hand was in everything. It hadn't been so long since I'd been a baby Christian on an island, praying for God to send somebody. First he'd sent Julie, who had pointed me in the right direction. She led me to T-Bone. T-Bone directed me to the kind of church and Bible study fellowship I needed. The church had connected me to David Platt, who had sent me to seminary and taught me how to study the Bible and pray. From there, God sent Tim LaFleur into my path, and that was a spiritual tsunami in my life. Meanwhile, he'd also sent the perfect woman, my soul mate, wife, and best friend.

As I work through my story, I realize over and over again how God sends people into our lives at just the right time. When I was begging God for someone to disciple me, he sent David. When I couldn't figure out what to do with my summer, God sent my friend Byron, who could testify to Tim's excellence as a disciple-maker. When I couldn't decide what to do about my relationship with Kandi, Tim was there to speak into my life the principles and discernment I needed to move forward and propose marriage.

We're never alone. Wherever we are, whatever we face, God will send someone to offer the wisdom and guidance we need. All we need to do is to be open and receptive. From the bottom of my heart, I thank the Lord for his grace and providence during a formative period of my ministerial life. I may have been Ignorance on Fire, but I discovered fire isn't a bad thing. As one of my favorite preachers, Leonard Ravenhill, used to say, "You don't have to advertise a fire; it advertises itself."

I was a walking billboard of God's grace.

Chapter 18

HE SPEAKS FROM THE WHIRLWIND

In 2005, I was a newlywed with a life not too far from perfect. I was in the city I loved with the bride I loved, and we were together on the campus where I was studying. Kandi had a job there. We also lived rent-free in the home of my grandfather, while he stayed with my parents.

I continued my preparation for some form of ministry—but what kind? I wasn't the typical seminary student. For one thing, I was receiving invitations to come and preach, sharing my story and a few magic tricks. It was so clear that God had taken nearly all of those opportunities away when I'd sunk back into addiction. Now, to my surprise, the phone began to ring again while I was in seminary. God was gradually restoring opportunities to serve him.

But those invitations created a bit of tension and resentment of me on campus. Here I was, still a new believer compared to many of them, still learning some of the basics of the faith—and yet I was already helping to finance my education through preaching engagements.

Some of the students questioned my speaking schedule. I can understand how some might have said, "Why should he get so many invitations? Why should his message be more valuable than ours? He's a new convert! This guy is sharing the gospel with tricks and gimmicks instead of sound theology."

It wasn't just the magic, of course. There was no "smoke and mirrors" when it came to my testimony, and I always felt that was the true heart of what I had to offer.

But I could sense the skepticism, and it played on my own vulnerabilities, because I still fought self-doubts. I still struggled with the old identity question. Who is Robby Gallaty?

Well, he was no longer an addict. He was no longer lost. He was a committed follower of Jesus Christ, and he was pursuing a full-time ministry. But was I good enough? Was I mature enough? And what kind of ministry would fit someone like me?

To be candid, I grew tired of having to apologize for my lack of depth when it came to Bible knowledge. I was learning as fast as I could. I was fully committed. What else was I supposed to do?

In one of the campus Bible studies, a student began teaching on James 3:1, which says, "Not many should become teachers, my brothers, because you know that we will receive a stricter judgment." He was hammering home the point about needing the maturity to teach. As he continued to talk, I noticed his hand kept sweeping in my direction, as if pointing me out. "Too many people rush out to preach and teach when they're not ready," he said. "They'll receive a stricter judgment." His eyes brushed across mine.

Maybe it was subconscious or maybe it was deliberate; for me, it seemed pretty clear where he was aiming his message. I sat and stewed, and at the end of the session, I wanted to confront him about it. "Do you have a problem with me, brother?" I asked. I only wanted to talk with him about it directly. But when you're six-and-a-half feet tall, you can be imposing without intending it. Several other students jumped in between us: "Come on now, Robby—let's stay calm."

I could only sigh in exasperation. I wasn't going to knock anyone out; I just wanted us to clear the air.

This kind of thing only added to my sense of alienation from the student body, other than my closest friends. The way I looked at it, everybody else had a head start in being "seasoned." I couldn't catch up with them. They were made for the pastorate, most of them. I felt like the apostle Paul when he said, "Last of all, as to one born at the wrong time, he also appeared to me" (1 Cor. 15:8).

Why wasn't I saved in college? Why did I have to endure drugs and alcohol? Why did I have to lose so many friends before I found Christ? Why did it take so long? I've learned since then that God's timing is impeccable. He may not be on *our* time, but he's always *on* time.

There are no accidents in the economy of God.

So, I decided, maybe God wasn't leading me in the direction of preaching regularly at a church. I could imagine a search committee interviewing me and wondering about my past, and whether it would stay in the past. I was a risk.

What made more sense was that I become a revival-type preacher. I had a powerful story to share, I connected well with lost people, and nobody had to worry about me in the long term. I'd be more like Billy Graham, traveling and maybe building an organization. I loved the message from 2 Chronicles, my first real sermon. The message of spiritual awakening was close to my heart.

I devoured sermons from preachers like Leonard Ravenhill, Paul Washer, and Paris Reidhead. Most of my time was spent studying the Great Awakenings in our country.

Whether it was the First Great Awakening with Edwards, Whitefield, and Wesley, the Second Great Awakening with Finney, Asbury, and Campbell, or the prayer revival that started in New York led by Jeremiah Lanphier, I yearned to see God do that again in America.

Traveling and speaking seemed like the avenue to bring about revival, and it best fit my gifts.

I told Kandi how and why I felt this way about my future, but she didn't really endorse that evaluation. Kandi has incredible discernment, and she's unlikely to make impulsive decisions the way I always have.

One of my best experiences was working with MissionLab, a seminary initiative built around the needs of New Orleans. Given the uniqueness of the city, MissionLab was a program for bringing in college students to do mission work, using our campus as the base. There were custom mission trips to the downtown area for groups of all sizes. While it functioned all year, summertime was, of course, the main hub of activity.

I was the camp pastor that summer—a natural fit because I knew the city and loved speaking to students. Whenever the seminary students caused me to doubt myself, it seemed as if God used the high school students to build me back up again.

As that summer began, I got involved in another prayer group. But this one was more ambitious. This one swung for the fences. Have you ever prayed for something so big that, if it happened, it could only be explained as divine intervention? Most of the time, if we're honest, we'll admit we lack the boldness. Maybe we're afraid God will ignore us, and our faith will be damaged. Yet great movements in Christian history have always begun when someone stepped up and dared to pray for the impossible.

For example, as recently as two centuries ago, world missions was all but nonexistent. This I knew from the story of William Carey, who gave his name to my college. Basically, churches worried about their own people and ignored Jesus' Great Commission, even though it was his final and greatest command.

Our marching orders are to make disciples of all nations. It's remarkable that 1,800 years after the Resurrection, there were almost no mission projects for doing that.

But in 1806, five students gathered in a grove of trees in Massachusetts to talk about that very idea. Why wasn't anyone trying to take the gospel to Asia or Africa? What could be done about that?

As they talked, the skies opened up and the rain began to pound on them. They took refuge under a haystack, strangely enough, and something about the whole experience, huddled together in prayer during the storm, got them fired up. Over time, those five students were all parts of pushing forward the world mission movement in fantastic ways.

One of them helped form the American Bible Society, translating the Bible into hundreds of other languages. Several of them formed a missions group that sent out 1,250 missionaries in its first fifty years. All of them had a vast impact on the world, and today a number of missions initiatives trace their beginnings back to those five students.

David Platt, Rob Wilton, and I wanted to reach New Orleans for Christ. Our prayer was to do something "out of the range" of our own capacity. We called our group "Out of Range for God," and the idea was to pray for God to do a mighty work that was out of our range, but not his. We asked eighteen others, mostly students, to be part of disciplined daily prayer time. On a given day, eighteen of those would pray for three people who would pray and fast—the "tip of the spear" for our prayer pursuit. All twenty-one prayed, but three of us at a time would be on our faces, praying and fasting with all our heart and soul.

Thursday was my day, for example. I remember I was going to be preaching on Thursdays to close out the MissionLab camp week. At the culmination of a week in a city where dependence upon God was a necessity, I would extend an invitation for people to come forward and make professions of faith, or commitments to missions and ministry. I prepared eagerly, knowing that eighteen guys were interceding before God on my behalf. They cried out for the power of God to fall on that meeting.

I felt God's presence that summer like never before, and I wasn't the only one. My study and prep time was phenomenal; my energy and faith levels were off the charts. The invitation we offered was like a dam breaking, with students pouring down to the front of the room before I even invited them. It was a bit like the West Virginia ski retreat, but even more powerful, because this time it was the result of earnest, dedicated prayer, and many of these students were committing themselves to missions and ministry.

It was the most anointed time of my life, and I remember feeling overwhelmed with emotion. With hundreds of high school students sensing the presence of God, I'd have to go backstage at times to get control of myself and the tears that were flowing down my face. Many nights I sat behind the curtain and wept tears of joy that God was using me again. I knew I was caught up in something God was doing, and there's no other feeling in life quite like that.

Our Out of Range prayer group was tapping into the heart of God for this city, and we began asking, "Does he want to do even more than this? Is what we're seeing only the beginning?" We felt a burden for the city we were in and for seeing it come to Christ in an incredible way.

What we visualized was something culminating in a huge revival at the Superdome, home of the New Orleans Saints and often the Super Bowl. Again and again we returned to that image of people streaming into the Dome and having God show up in power. But the summer was now winding down, and it was time to begin preparing for the fall semester.

If we'd watched the news closely, we'd have learned that meteorologists were following the development of something called Tropical Storm 12, over the Bahamas, on the morning of August 24. It was hurricane season.

Two hours before making landfall in Florida the next morning, this tropical storm was upgraded to hurricane status. The name assigned to it was Katrina. After entering the Gulf, it moved from Category Three status to Category Five in only nine hours, and things got serious.

On August 29, it made landfall on the shores of Louisiana.

At the outset of those events, our prayer group capped off the summer by holding a retreat in Pass Christian, Mississippi, about an hour from New Orleans. Some of our wives gathered back in town at my home. We went to the retreat center to celebrate, continue praying together, and, as the Spirit led us, repent of sin and rededicate ourselves to God. It was a truly wonderful time, but that wasn't surprising—serious prayer has the effect of bonding people together like nothing else.

I thought about the previous summer, when I'd been with Tim LaFleur in New Mexico. That had been a huge growth experience for me. This summer, praying with the guys had offered me another leap forward. I'd seen what God could do when his people took prayer seriously instead of simply giving it lip service.

This was a time of joy, of summing up our summer experience before moving into another school year. We had no idea how our lives were about to be disrupted.

As the storm continued to get worse, I remained convinced to ride it out. That's what you do if you're from the Gulf Coast—I was too Cajun to go back home, get Kandi, and evacuate. Some of the others felt the same way, and we decided to stay the course.

But Kandi overruled me. I checked in with her on the phone, and she said, "Come get me, Robby. I've got the TV on, and this thing looks serious. We need to evacuate."

She's always the voice of reason in my life, so I didn't argue. I made the short drive back home. We packed our belongings in one suitcase, along with two to three days' worth of clothing. Then we grabbed our dog Gracie and took off, leaving behind our other car, our wedding gifts, our pictures, and our videos. What we thought would be two to three days, however, lasted forever. There would be no home to come back to.

———

We figured Denham Springs, east of Baton Rouge, was a safe enough distance. Kandi's family was there, and they took us in. Along with the rest of the world, we watched the reports in horror, with Katrina thrashing across the coast and then breaching the New Orleans hurricane surge protection in more than fifty places. The levees burst. Eventually, more than 1,800 people would lose their lives.

For someone like me who had lived so much of my life in that city, the images of the French Quarter were devastating. New Orleans had seemed ancient and somehow immortal; the places I'd known so well were now swept away in the floodwaters. People were on rooftops, praying for rescue. Thousands were in distress. The truth was laid bare: nothing on this earth lasts. Anything can be gone in an instant.

We saw those shots of the Superdome, swarming with evacuees, and I thought about all our prayers for a revival there. Really, God? This was the answer to our prayer? It was the exact opposite of everything we'd prayed about.

Denham Springs lost its power, but we continued to watch on an old four-inch, battery-operated TV set, found by my father-in-law. It was day three when I was finally able to talk to my parents. "Thank God you're safe," my mom said.

"You, too," I said. "I've prayed for you guys. What have you heard about home?"

"We just found out we've lost everything."

"What? Everything?"

"Ten to twelve feet of water to the roof in our home. It's all destroyed. And Robby—your home, where you've been staying—there was an oil spill at the refinery."

She was talking about Chalmette's Murphy Oil facility, where the storm brought down a huge tank, and thousands of gallons of oil gushed into the water. Everything was contaminated, and we wouldn't be allowed to go near our home for months. All that we'd left behind was gone forever. Along with my stuff being kept by my parents. Pictures of my whole childhood; collectables; old mementos; basketball videos; everything.

I felt worse for my dad. Dad's whole family heritage was lost. Multiply these stories by the whole population of New Orleans and the vicinity. Small towns were destroyed. People disappeared and were never accounted for. You couldn't feel too sorry for yourself, because someone you knew had it even worse.

A weather event had turned our world upside down. It was impossible not to wonder what God was doing, and whether he'd heard a single thing we'd prayed. These are the times when our faith is tested.

I thought about that interrupted retreat in Gulfport, in which we prayed, sang, celebrated, and drew closer together than ever, sure that God was doing something. We believe he's always moving, that nothing happens for no reason. So what was this natural disaster all about?

It's hard to say for certain. God works in ways we don't always understand, and where he hasn't clearly revealed his purposes, we shouldn't claim to know them. Nonetheless, in a sense, this storm felt like a powerful, God-glorifying, but very unexpected answer to our prayer.

We'd asked him to move in a way so big it would be out of our range. And that's just what he did. He scattered our group all over the world with that hurricane. Without it, as close as we'd grown, most of us probably would've stayed close by.

We had a burden for New Orleans. God had a burden for the world, and that's exactly where this storm sent us.

Katrina forced us out of our range. God was saying, "Give up your small ambitions." He moved in such a large way that not only was it out of our range, but we couldn't even see it for a good while. Over the years I would chart the movements of my friends and see how God was using them everywhere, powerfully, exponentially—because of that storm.

We had envisioned a great, old-fashioned revival that would shake the city of New Orleans. We imagined people crying out in repentance at the Superdome. That had come to pass, in a way, but the Lord's ear was tuned into the cries of people throughout the world. This was something I'd struggled with from the very beginning: We serve a "big picture" God. No matter how much we try to dream big, it's never big enough to outdistance what God wants to do through us.

———

New Orleans would heal over time. Bourbon Street would hear the sound of jazz once again—not to mention our Saints would go on to win their first Super Bowl, an answered prayer for every native. God moved in more ways than one, of course. He mobilized believers across the world to respond in love and compassion. There were stories of people finding Christ in the midst of crisis. And then there was the Out of Range group; we were driven out of our range and into God's.

In the book of Job, there's a verse that says that God speaks from the whirlwind. We know that to be true. There's another verse, however, that describes our situation even better. God says, "I scattered them with a whirlwind among all the nations that they had not known" (Zech. 7:14 ESV).

That's a verse about the terrible days when the people of Israel and Judah were scattered in defeat, but it holds an amazing truth: Scattering his people is one of God's choice tactics for advancing the kingdom. He will do whatever it takes to get his people into "all the nations that they had not known."

Christianity spread in the first century when the Romans drove Jewish believers out of their home country. Wherever they went, seeds of churches were scattered on new ground; then God sent Paul to water and tend the new fellowships.

Then there was the Haystack Prayer Meeting, another occasion when the skies opened up, a storm came, and God scattered young men across the world.

We figured all this out eventually, and we could only shake our heads.

I would never suggest that Katrina, with all its death and devastation, was all about us. I still grieve for the lives lost and the damage done. But I serve a Romans 8:28 God who uses all things for his glory, tragedies included. He speaks from the whirlwind, and he turns tragedy into triumph.

Chapter 19

PROVIDENCE

In the wake of a raging storm, we sat in the darkened home of Kandi's parents and checked in with our friends by phone—wondering when we'd be able to recharge these mobile phones; wondering if life would ever be normal again.

Rob Wilton, one of my closest friends, was with his parents in Spartanburg, South Carolina. He told us there was no power problem in the Carolinas, and there was plenty of room. "I talked to Dad," he said. "He wants me to tell you and Kandi to pack your things and come live here in South Carolina."

It seemed like a big step, even from our reduced circumstances. We were two Louisiana natives who were now homeless, and Spartanburg was more than six hundred miles away. But we prayed about it and decided this was what God wanted us to do. On our sixth day in Denham Springs, we repacked the suitcase, put gas in the car, and headed for the East Coast.

On the road there were buses and vans packed with shell-shocked people who had lost everything and now depended upon the kindness of strangers. They peered out the windows of their vehicles, their lives now reduced to open questions. Kandi and I prayed for them, asking God to move the hearts of his people in response.

The word in the Bible is *diaspora*—the dispersion of people outward, in every direction, due to crisis. The population of Louisiana decreased by 300,000 after the storm. Some of the people came back during the following months and years; many never did. They went to Texas or Georgia, Arkansas or Florida, and churches everywhere opened their doors to the displaced. People created new lives for themselves.

Our fellow seminary students, as well as the professors, were spread in every direction, too. But Dr. Kelley and the staff responded beautifully, moving many of the classes to the Internet and extension centers. Eighty-five percent of the students moved seamlessly to online classes or plugged in at a seminary extension center. Within weeks, churches were sending people to clean up the campus and prepare it for the following semester, and the Southern Baptist Convention made a huge, sacrificial donation to the seminary and to humanitarian aid for the city.

We all know there are people who love to condemn the church, saying it's "full of hypocrites" and that kind of thing. There's even more scorn for old-fashioned denominations such as the SBC. But I've seen how these crises become the church's finest hour, again and again. And the cooperation of Baptist churches makes immense generosity available. God moves the hearts of his people, and they rise to the occasion, showing sacrificial love and compassion. Kandi and I were soon to experience this ourselves.

It was good to see Rob and Annabeth Wilton again. Rob is a Southern, African-American Cajun, by his own description—a unique guy. His mom and dad are from South Africa but came to New Orleans for seminary. Rob, his brother

Greg, and his sister Shelley, were all born on the New Orleans Seminary campus. Then he spent his high school and college years in South Carolina, when his dad became the pastor of First Baptist Spartanburg.

Like me, he was a college basketball player. He and I worked with MissionLab and prayed together in the Out of Range group. God has extended his range since then through an opportunity to be an NFL chaplain for the Saints, as well as preaching all over the world. Rob planted Vintage Church in New Orleans in 2008, bringing a new ray of hope to a city trying to rise again from the floodwaters. He was one of the few who went back.

One other thing—Rob's dad, Don Wilton, was Billy Graham's pastor for the last two decades of Dr. Graham's life. In retirement, Dr. Graham joined Don's church even though he lived more than an hour up the road near Asheville, North Carolina. He respected Rob's dad that much, and looked to him for counsel and encouragement during his final hours.

When we arrived in Spartanburg, the Wiltons received us with open arms. I honestly don't know what we'd have done otherwise, but this episode was clearly a key piece in God's plan for us all along. It was his way of finally showing me the range of ministry he had set out for me.

———

Kandi and I settled in to a small trailer the church made available, and Dr. Wilton immediately let us know he was going to put us to work at First Baptist. I was all for that. He knew we needed to be busy, and in particular, busy with ministry. What we didn't need was to brood over what we'd lost and why God had chosen such a perplexing way to respond to our prayers.

There was also an immediate question to address. Two months after Katrina, in October of that year, Rob and I had scheduled a mission trip to Indonesia with David Platt, my first overseas mission trip. I'd really looked forward to it—one of my first true mission experiences—but now I couldn't imagine such a thing. I told Kandi, "I'm pretty sure I need to pull out of that trip. It just seems wrong to leave you here in Spartanburg, when we've both lost so much. We need to be together right now, don't you think?"

Kandi didn't hesitate to vote me down. She's the most supportive wife and ministry partner imaginable, but she won't hesitate to give me her honest take. "Robby, this is a trip God planned," she said. "He knew the hurricane would come, but he called you to that mission. So I don't think you should back out of it."

I prayed about the trip and came to the conclusion that she was right, especially since she assured me she would be fine in Spartanburg. I had to believe God opened the door for the mission trip, and he would close it if he had other plans for me. David, Rob, and I traveled on to Indonesia, and to this day, I'm so grateful we made that trip and I didn't miss an important spiritual marker in my life.

Crisis times tend to focus us inward. We become absorbed in our own problems and changing plans. It's healthy to break out of all that and get involved and visit the front lines of kingdom work. This whole episode of my life was about learning to depend upon God and his providence—this was a perspective-changing moment.

Our task was to teach in a Christian seminary. Indonesia is a fascinating place. It holds the fourth largest population group in the world, the largest Muslim population in the world, and it's made up of 17,000 islands that stretch across an area wider than the United States. With all of that, the gospel is on the move in that country. As you visit God's people there, you can sense the intensity that's in the air when God's Spirit is moving.

But it wasn't exactly the calmest place to visit after our storm. Muslims were on the move as much as the gospel was. There was violence in the air. Indonesia has 267 million people, 88 percent of them Muslim.[3]

That's a lot of radicalized people, and a Christian seminary is an obvious target.

Huge, eager crowds showed up to listen to us speak. The local people were thrilled to hear from their American visitors. They came by bus, by motorcycle, and by foot, many walking great distances. They came through danger and strife, and as we spoke, every eye was on us. Every ear was tuned in to our words. Everyone who teaches or preaches loves to have an audience that is one hundred percent attentive. This was what it looked like when people were famished for sound teaching and the solid meat of God's Word.

As we finished our teaching segment, I turned to Rob and said, "They've heard what we have to say—now, if it's okay, I'd like to hear what *they* have to say."

We explained that it would be our deep privilege to hear their personal stories, and we turned the microphone over to our hosts. We listened just as attentively as they described death threats to those who wanted to follow Christ. We heard a woman speak of being beaten by her father with a chair, almost to death, because she had left her Islamic faith.

Everything the early Christians experienced in Rome and Jerusalem, these people were now living through in Indonesia.

People in our audience had lost their homes not to hurricanes, but to hatred. They had built churches and seen them bombed to rubble. They had been deserted by friends and family. And the more suffering they endured, the deeper their love for Christ grew. Like the apostle Paul, they found it a privilege to share in the sufferings of Christ.

There was a graduation ceremony, and David Platt was the guest speaker. We found out that things worked a little differently than at an American seminary graduation. To receive a diploma, these people had to plant a church in a Muslim community, then bear witness as five new believers were baptized.

Needless to say, we forgot all about Louisiana and our own challenges. We had a new set of heroes. The ceremony recognized two planters who hadn't made it—they were martyrs to the cause of the kingdom of God, and while they didn't receive a seminary diploma, they were now receiving a crown of glory. It was incredibly moving.

Was there a message in all this for me? I felt certain there was, at this crucial point in my life. I had faced a little bit of adversity, and Jesus wanted to know if I was really ready to take up my cross and follow him—out of my range. The three of us felt inadequate and humbled.

We flew home, and I was delighted to be back with Kandi in Spartanburg; I had so much to tell her. But there was also a lot of work to be done. Dr. Wilton had a plan for Rob and me in the church.

I was glad to help, but I didn't look at it as valuable experience for me personally. After all, I wasn't going to work in local churches; I wasn't the type. My spiritual gifts and talents, along with my unique story, seemed to suggest I needed to be an itinerant preacher, somebody who traveled and spoke. I'd now done that in Southeast Asia, as well as any number of places in my own country. Life on the road as a revival preacher seemed like my destiny.

Now Dr. Wilton told me what he had in mind. "Robby," he said, "I'm going to give you a crash course in everyday church ministry. You've learned a lot of information in seminary, but you're about to learn by doing."

The plan was that I'd work in a different area of ministry every week, shadowing the staff member who handled that part of things. The church had a senior adult pastor, and I took a week to work with him. I'd never thought about the specific needs of an aging congregation. I really enjoyed that week.

Then came outreach visitation. I visited the homes of membership prospects, people who had expressed an interest in our church. Making those connections was enjoyable, and I could see the skills required in making a good impression on a church visit.

The associate pastor took me with him to visit the hospitals one week. The music minister showed me how much was involved in preparing to lead worship through song—more than I had ever imagined. The week for college and student ministry was a great week.

I began to realize that I enjoyed all of these things. And what came across clearly was that the connections I made, for example, with the teenagers and college students, were connections I really wanted to build on. The word for that is *relationship*.

Suddenly a new truth was driven home for me: a traveling preacher doesn't have relationships with that kind of durability—he moves along like the wind, from place to place, never lingering. And we need people who do that—people good at scattering seeds, while others water and tend. I was looking at a ministry in which I'd never see the full harvest.

Wow. This was one of those times when I felt my whole understanding of myself changing and rearranging, much like when Tim LaFleur had explained to me that faith was not about my strength, but God's.

A local church is an outpost of the kingdom of God, and it's all about the fields and their ripeness. The church sows, it reaps, it nurtures. I realized how much I wanted to see that in others, even as I was seeing that growth in myself. I wanted to be a disciple who makes disciples.

Spending those weeks in local church ministry helped me understand the power of what is done through personal relationships that endure over time. The body of Christ finds and uses its gifts to build up one another. My particular part in that might be to proclaim God's Word, but I would be proclaiming it to listeners I knew personally and cared about. I could preach to their needs. I could minister to them, face-to-face.

There was something else. I saw firsthand how powerful the love of a church fellowship can be. For three months I learned about these ministries and made new friends. The people at First Baptist were receptive and incredibly loving to us at such a fragile time in our young marriage. We'd lost everything. What were we going to do?

We were going to learn dependence upon our heavenly Father and the power of his forever family, the church. We needed to trust him to provide for us. Kandi no longer had a seminary job. We had school loans and other financial responsibilities, and just a few hundred dollars in the bank. I had a few preaching invitations here and there, but we had no other source of income. I remember the two of us getting down on our knees in the trailer, committing ourselves to trust God for our finances. *Lord,* we prayed, *we put all our faith in you, and we won't worry about our finances. No matter what our checkbook says, we're going to give you 10 percent off the top of everything that comes in.*

My parents were staying in Houston, the home of Exxon, where Mom had worked. They worried more about us than we did. I'd patiently explain, "Mom, Dad, God will provide. He has led us this far, and he won't desert us now."

"I just don't know, Robby," Mom or Dad would say. "How can you be sure? Why don't you guys move to Houston to be by us?"

"Mom," I assured her, "we'll be fine."

There was an old-fashioned tent revival in Union, South Carolina, a working-class town. Dr. Wilton preached it, and Rob and I attended. On the first night, Dr. Wilton leaned over to his son and said, "Rob, you're up, brother." Rob got up to speak to the crowd, and he talked a bit about Katrina. He said, "The truth is, I didn't lose as much as others—but my friend here lost it all," and he pointed to me. "We're committed to trusting the Lord."

The next day, Kandi and Annabeth came along with us, and this time I got the "you're up, brother" assignment. I stood and told my life story, how I was saved from drugs and alcohol, and what we'd been through with the hurricane. I said, "I have lost everything I own twice, but Kandi and I know God will provide. We're completely trusting in him."

After I spoke, one of the local pastors stood up and said, "I'd like to say a word about the offering tonight. I didn't tell them this, so they know nothing about it, but everything you give tonight will go to the Gallatys and Wiltons as they put their lives back together. God is going to take care of them, but one of the ways he's going to do that is right now, through your generosity."

Kandi and I looked at each other, stunned. We fought tears. After the services that night, Dr. Wilton arrived home with a cardboard box filled with money. When he turned over the box, a mound of money filled the living room. With tears streaming down our faces, we counted seven thousand dollars. It seemed like a million to us. It was a joy to talk to my parents again and say, "Remember when I told you God would provide?"

In addition to the love offering that night, money also came in from the wonderful people of Spartanburg. Those three months built our faith on the assurance that, no matter what happens in life, God is greater, and he will use it for his purposes. We lived in a trailer during that autumn feeling like millionaires. We'd never felt so confident of God's care for us.

———

"Kandi," I said one evening, "I have something to talk about with you."

"What now?"

"I think God is calling me to pastoral ministry. In a local church. Don't faint."

"Oh, I won't," she said, matter-of-factly. "I came to that conclusion when I met you. I was just wondering if *you* would ever figure it out."

"What? How could you have known that?"

"I know *you*, Robby. I know who you are, and that tells me how God is likely to use you. And I've watched you fall in love with serving a church."

This was one of those times when I wished God had let me in on what was going on, at least before he told my wife. Then again, she has a gift for discernment, and I don't know what I'd do without her by my side to keep me from making mistake after mistake.

I told her, "Let's pray about this. I know how I feel about what God wants me to do, but I really want to be sure I'm right. I need to make sure I'm not operating on emotion, but hearing what he's really saying to me."

"I agree," she smiled. "We'll keep praying."

"So I'm not going to put my résumé out or anything like that, or go out seeking a position. I'm going to wait on the Lord, continue praying, and if he opens that door, and a church extends a call, then I'll follow what he wants me to do from there."

There's an incredible freedom in trusting the providence of God. How much anxiety do we carry on our shoulders everywhere we go, because we think everything in life depends upon us? We talk a good game when it comes to faith, but when it comes to dependence, most of us have room to grow.

Jesus tells us the hairs on our head are numbered; God has this. Once we actually believe that and live in accordance with it, life is totally different. All that space in our heads, once devoted to full-time worrying, is freed up for so many things. We can live creatively and enjoy the ride, and we're able to hear from God so much more clearly.

That's not the same as living carelessly without thinking and planning. When I was a brand-new Christian, I thought I didn't need to put together sermon plans for a ski retreat. I would walk out and trust the Holy Spirit to give me the words. It was like giving him the wheel, but going to sleep in the backseat.

That's not how it works, of course. Life is a cooperative venture between God and you. That's the beauty of being his servant—he guides, but he gives us a mind and the gifts to be obedient and participate in the process.

Toward the end of 2005—the year of the great flood—I was finally beginning to learn how to do that. My identity as a child of God was finally crystallizing. I had a conviction forming within me that God wanted me to be a local church pastor. I'd bonded with that idea through my experiences in Spartanburg. Just the same, I continued to wait on the Lord to confirm what I was feeling through the offer of a real opportunity to follow that calling.

I didn't have to wait for long.

Chapter 20

NEW HOME, NEW FAMILY

God used our three months in Spartanburg for more than healing. Kandi and I had tremendous opportunities for spiritual growth. We faced our first financial crisis and learned what it meant to trust God through it. I bonded with the idea of pastoral ministry—a complete change of thinking for me. I even went on a faith-expanding mission trip.

Now it was late November, and we were headed back westward for Thanksgiving in Houston with my folks. I'd also received an invitation to stop in Morgan City, Louisiana, to preach a sermon on Sunday.

On the way home, I thought about the opportunity to spend time with my parents. Throughout all my struggles, they'd been there for me. They could have walked away forever after I stole from them. Other parents might have given up on someone like me. Instead, they were models of unconditional love when I needed mercy and tough love when I needed correction.

My parents had given me their all. The greatest and only gift I could give in return, other than my love and respect, was to continue to share the gospel with them.

They'd watched the progress of my faith with surprise and a growing respect, but it was also puzzling to them. My passion and commitment to Christ weren't much like the faith they had practiced all their lives.

My sister Lori had been more receptive. She'd come to know Jesus in 2005, at Creedmoor Presbyterian, when I preached there once again. It would soon be destroyed by Katrina, but on this day, that church was very much alive, and the Spirit moved there.

When I gave an invitation at the close of my sermon, Lori walked down the aisle. Somehow I managed to pray with her, as my eyes filled with tears. My sister, who had always supported me, would now join me in eternal life.

During my time in Spartanburg, I checked in with my parents over the phone each week. I talked about my relationship with Jesus whenever possible, always in a non-confrontational way, with my dad. He listened patiently, more or less. I wanted so badly for him to see what it meant to have a living faith, to know and walk with Christ day by day. How could I show him the difference it made? Finally I said, "Dad, wouldn't you agree that you and I study the same Bible?"

"Sure," he said.

"So doesn't it make sense that if we're in the same book, we should both be learning about our faith at church?"

"Makes sense to me. But I was told not to read the Bible growing up."

"Do you still feel that way?" I asked.

"No."

"Well, let's try something. You go to your church and I'll go to my church each week. Then, every Sunday, we can compare what we learned."

He had no objections.

One week later, we talked again. He talked about Houston, where he and Mom were getting settled after having to leave their home. I brought him up-to-date on our experience in Spartanburg and how the church was reaching out to us. Then I said, "So, Dad, we were going to compare what we learned in church. Did you attend this week?"

"Well, yeah, but to tell the truth, I was tired. I guess my mind was elsewhere. I don't really remember anything that was discussed."

"Don't worry about it; I'll tell you mine. I heard about the time Jesus multiplied a boy's lunch, and he said, 'I am the bread of life.' I learned how the loaves of bread represent our satisfaction in life." I shared the main points of Dr. Wilton's teaching.

"I see," said Dad. "Well, I guess that was a pretty good sermon."

"It left me a lot to think about this week."

The next week I raised the topic again and asked Dad about church. He said, "Um, well, we had a visiting priest. I remember the speaker system was lousy, and—well, that's all I got, to be honest."

I told him about the sermon I'd heard, which had all kinds of implications for daily life.

The third week, I could tell Dad had tried a little harder to listen. He said, "The priest told a joke about a chicken and an egg."

"That's funny. But what did you learn from the Bible, Dad?"

He sighed and responded, "Bible? I don't remember anything from the Bible." There was a long pause. He thought a moment and said, "In fact, I've gone to Mass my entire life, because it's what you do, but I haven't learned anything from the Bible."

I didn't know what to say. The honesty from my Dad was raw and authentic. My response was, "We can't change the past, but we can do something about the future. Let's work on changing that."

This was the beginning of God softening my dad's heart. He knew I was learning things that had to do with how I lived, and I'm sure he could see the difference in me. But he couldn't understand why he didn't have the same experience. Church was a duty; he and Mom had never really thought about it any other way. And they were suspicious of "religious fanatics" who carried their Bibles around and badgered people. I was trying to help them see something different: a practical, passionate faith that goes with you, instead of staying inside with the pews and stained glass windows.

———

Kandi and I stopped at Immanuel Baptist Church and had a wonderful visit. Morgan City bills itself as "right in the middle of everywhere." It's a bayou town, an hour from my hometown and an hour from Kandi's. Morgan City had come through Hurricane Katrina without much devastation. As a matter of fact, it was proud to be one of the first places to take in refugees from the flooding in New Orleans.

The church was without a pastor, and they'd asked me to preach earlier, before the hurricane. Back then, however, they knew I had no interest in pastoring, and I didn't consider myself a candidate.

The church was small, with about sixty-five in attendance, but they were very receptive. We felt the presence of the Holy Spirit as I spent time with them.

The next day, they called to invite me to be their pastor. I thanked them, told them I was honored, and told them I would pray about it. I called Tim LaFleur shortly after.

"What do you think, Brother Tim?" I asked. "Be honest. In many ways, I'm still a new believer—even a new husband. Am I ready to be a pastor?"

"Well, you're a new believer, but you've had your share of experiences," he said. "You've shown a lot of growth, you've managed adversity well, and God is really moving in your life. I feel this is probably the right time for you to pastor a group of people, but also to be shepherded *by* them."

He made a great point. I knew I would need them as much as they needed me. In Spartanburg, one of the things I realized is that ministry is a two-way street, if it's going to be real.

"God blesses you as he blesses people through you," Tim said. "And you and Kandi have gone through a lot over the past four months. Settling down in one place will be good for you and her."

As Kandi and I prayed, I sensed God directing me to accept the call at Morgan City. She had a good feeling about it as well. We called the committee at Morgan City and told them we were ready to talk about my being the pastor of Immanuel.

In Houston, my parents were glad to see us. We had a delicious Thanksgiving dinner, Gallaty-style. But during the cooking, Dad was given the assignment of going out to find some groceries. I told him I'd drive him there.

We jumped in the car and backed down the driveway. As we were riding along, I leaned over and said, "Dad, let me ask you a question. This storm has been one of the worst we've ever been through. We both lost our homes. But we could have lost our lives, like thousands did. Have you ever thought about that? What would have happened if you'd died in the storm? Do you know for sure that you would have spent eternity in heaven with Christ?"

"Well, I don't know . . ."

"You don't know where you would spend eternity?"

"No," he said, "I don't."

He was silent, but he wasn't changing the subject. I could tell he was struggling within himself—that this was part of a long-time struggle as God had pursued him. I would never have raised this subject unless I felt moved by the Spirit that the timing was right.

I continued, "It's not a matter of what church you go to, Dad—what denomination, what kind of water they sprinkle you with. It's something between you and God, and it's a free gift. That's the incredible thing about it. He offers this to you, the gift of salvation, and you need only say yes. And I think you know, just from our talks, you receive a whole lot more than a ticket to heaven. This is a daily relationship with Christ. He fills you with his Holy Spirit today to live in the kingdom. It's the peace and purpose that has completely turned my life around."

He nodded thoughtfully, and I could see the emotion he was feeling.

"Dad, do you think you'd like to pray to Jesus today, ask him to forgive your sins, and put your complete trust in him? You don't need a priest, or even me. It's between you and God, your decision to follow him and to have new life and assurance of your salvation."

He nodded, and his eyes met mine. "I don't know what to say," he said. "I've never prayed like that."

"I can help you with that," I said. And as we parked the car, we sat, my hand on his shoulder, and I led him in a prayer of commitment to Christ. When it was over, I gave him a big hug and clung to him for a few seconds. We just sat silently for a while; then we picked up those groceries and headed home for a truly special Thanksgiving.

———

During the next year, I began my ministry as a pastor. Morgan City was a friendly town, and I came to love those people very quickly. The town is diverse, with French, Spanish, Italian, German, Dutch, Native American, and African American heritages mingling together—a microcosm of our world today. I got acquainted with those who were our members and those who weren't.

As I mentioned, the church had gotten down to sixty-five people for Sunday morning worship. This could be the reason they took a chance on a first-time pastor who had been sober for only three years. The Immanuel folks wanted to reach new believers and see their church grow; they just needed someone to lead them in that direction.

My basic strategy was 2 Timothy 2:2, which says, "What you have heard from me in the presence of many witnesses, commit to faithful men who will be able to teach others also."

These words were written from the apostle Paul to Timothy, whom he had already discipled. Now Paul was challenging his younger protégé to pass on what he had learned—the biblical model of disciple-making.

I chose a handful of our men to pour my life into; Kandi did the same with a group of women. We knew this was the best possible investment of our time as church leaders. We taught, trained, and challenged those in our group to look toward multiplying their growth by starting new groups. During our first year, we saw more people make decisions for Christ than were attending when we arrived.

More than once I heard people say, "It feels like we're living the book of Acts." There was an electric intensity in the air, the feeling like no other that means the Spirit of God is on the move.

It was there I met my prayer partner, Jody Blaylock. He was a modern-day E. M. Bounds or Andrew Murray. Jody visited our church one Sunday morning. He had moved to Morgan City from New Orleans after Hurricane Katrina, so he was also new in town. We immediately hit it off. He asked me a question that would change my prayer life forever.

He asked, "Do you have a prayer partner?"

"Yes, I love to pray," was my response.

"I understand that, but do you have someone you pray with regularly who holds you accountable to pray?"

I had never been asked that before. Sure, I prayed with friends in my grandfather's home shortly after getting saved, and with David every week on the steps of the chapel at New Orleans Seminary, but I never had anyone with whom I regularly prayed.

Jody invited me to meet him the next morning at 7:30 a.m. in the McDonald's parking lot. I assumed we would meet up to drink coffee, eat an Egg McMuffin, and talk for a while. But I was wrong. Heading into the McDonald's, I noticed someone motioning to me from inside a vehicle. It was Jody. When I sat down, he asked if he could call his friend Doug to pray with us. "Sure," I said.

We never made it inside the restaurant that day. We prayed in his car in the parking lot for almost an hour. After finishing his prayer, Jody concluded by saying, "Okay, brother, I'll see you next week—same time, same place."

I walked back to my truck saying to myself, "What about the coffee and the Egg McMuffin?"

For the next four months, we prayed together every Monday morning in the McDonald's parking lot. Later, because of changes in our schedules, we prayed by phone rather than in person.

I was learning so much at this time. I thanked God for showing me I was designed for the pastorate despite all my self-doubt. And I knew that wherever the Lord may lead us in the future, the first subject we'd raise would be discipleship—discipleship and missions would define us, and we'd be all about building fully committed followers of Jesus.

Kandi and I went on to have a wonderful three years in Morgan City before accepting a call to Brainerd Baptist Church in Chattanooga, Tennessee.

As busy as those early years of ministry were, I thought frequently about my mom. My dad and my sister had come to faith, but there was unfinished business in my family. I just knew that sooner or later, Mom would be saved as well. I would keep praying until it happened.

I called Mom regularly and told her all the exciting news from Morgan City—people coming to Christ, long dormant faith being reignited, marriages being redeemed, young people sharing their faith at school for the first time. I wanted badly to paint a picture for her of this world of a living, redemptive Jesus. But she remained resistant.

Mom never quite seemed to grasp the need of every man and woman for salvation. She would say, "Robby, you *needed* to be saved. You had so many issues in your life. I'm glad you found God, because it's been good for you. But I'm just fine the way I am."

"It's been good for me because it's good for everyone, Mom. It's *necessary* for everyone."

N.B. For dad

"Robby," she said, "I've always been a good person. I've never gotten into any trouble, and I've been in church all my life."

"Of course. But going to church doesn't make you a Christian. And being good is not going to work. The issue of salvation is living up to God's perfect standard. And nobody in this world can do that—not based on how we live, even if it seems that by some standard, we're 'good' people. How good is good enough to be saved?"

"I don't know."

I continued, "The standard for God is infinitely high—it's perfection. You can be the best wife, the best mother, the best anything, but you'd still stand before God as a sinner—just like me, just like everybody. Mom, I'm off drugs. I try to be a good husband. I help people. But I'm no more righteous in God's eyes now, based on my actions, than I was when I was utterly messed up! I'm just more socially acceptable. When I stand before God, that won't cut it."

"That's hard for me to believe, Robby."

"There must be a moment when you accept the gift of God, through his grace, and go from death into life. What Jesus did on the cross is create a way for you and me to be fully forgiven. I said I wasn't any more righteous *by my actions*, but now, in God's eyes, I'm completely accepted *because of Jesus' finished work on the cross*. He lived the life I couldn't live and died the death I should have died. He traded his perfection for my sin. Yours, too."

By nothing else but her patient love and the work of God, she listened. She just couldn't see it. All I could do for her was to keep praying.

God was answering all along, because he was nurturing the seeds that had been planted. And one day in 2010, the harvest came. She was listening to a song at Spring Baptist

For dad

Church in Texas—the gospel song, "Born Again," by Ron Hamilton. I'd never have guessed God would use a song. He moves in mysterious ways! Seeds send forth their shoots and break the ground in their own time.

In that moment as the lyrics to the song came across, she simply believed. *Praise God.*

Here's what I learned.

Once I had confronted my parents and tried to argue them into salvation. That was a terrible idea.

Then I had gently reasoned with them, and that had worked at least a little better. No one got angry. And finally, through our conversations and his own reflection, Dad entered the family of God.

For Lori, it had been during a sermon in a tiny church. The words of Scripture, the Spirit moving in a worship service, and the voice of her brother—God had used these things to draw her to himself.

And for my Mom, music was the vehicle.

For everyone, it's something different. But ultimately it's one thing—the Spirit of God bringing people to conviction, repentance, and surrender to the love of Christ. We can be obedient and plant seeds, but the Spirit provides the water and the sunlight. All those years I felt my mother wasn't taking in a word I said; we couldn't connect. But at the proper time, the Holy Spirit spoke, and she responded. I learned a lesson in patience.

———

Years later, I had the incredible privilege of baptizing my father, my mother, and my sister on the same day, in Chattanooga, Tennessee. They visited often after I accepted a call to Brainerd Baptist Church.

One weekend, I revisited a question that was avoided years before because of our Catholic heritage: "What about following through with baptism now that each of you are saved?"

To my surprise, Mom spoke up first, "I'm ready."

On a Sunday evening, the three of them—Mom, Dad, and Lori—came forward in white robes, symbolizing their new purity as believers in Christ. All of them were smiling, the warmth of God's love filled the room, and I couldn't help but think of how far we'd come as a family. I'd been a drug addict. I'd stolen thousands of dollars from these people, the ones who loved me more than anyone else on the face of this earth. I knew I'd hurt Lori, too. Yet all of that was gone, covered by the blood of Jesus.

The past was nothing more than a marker to show us what God could do; all our tears were wiped away. All our heartache was pain well spent, if it could lead us to a moment this much like heaven.

My long search for a true identity had led me to the one identity that matters: that of a child of God.

I grinned at Dad, Mom, and Lori, and they beamed back—maybe a little nervously. I don't think any of them were crazy about being the center of attention in a large worship center. They'd have been so much more comfortable sitting around the table at Galatoire's, back in New Orleans, sharing a dish of shrimp and crab sardou and arguing about which movie to see. Maybe someday we'd do that again.

But they understood what this moment meant. Now we were whole. We were new creations, bound together by his kingdom and his love.

We'd been a good family, to be sure—a loving family, a circle of four who never gave up on one another. By social standards, an outstanding household. But now we were something more. By the standards of heaven, we were redeemed, pure and spotless in God's eyes, rescued, and part of the great forever family.

Mom, Dad, and Lori never gave up on me. When others turned their backs, they never did. God used them to save me from the toughest times of my life. But little did we know he was saving me so that one day he would save them.

I said a silent prayer of gratitude to God in that moment. I told him the rest of my life would be a sustained act of loving, grateful service to him.

Then I motioned my father to step into the cool water with me. I grabbed his hand as he entered.

AFTERWORD

After reading my life story, you may be thinking your life is different than mine. Maybe you've never struggled with alcohol or drugs, or maybe you have but not to the extent of the addiction I had. Regardless, we all share the same sin problem that can't be fixed by our own good works or meritorious actions. Every one of us needs a Savior to set us free and make us whole. If you've never surrendered your life to Jesus completely, I want to encourage you to do that now. The joy, peace, fulfillment, and satisfaction you've been searching for is found in him alone.

Some of the common rebuttals I've heard from people hesitant to submit their lives to Christ are:

"Robby, you don't know what I've done."

"Robby, you don't know where I've been."

"You don't know the pain I've caused others."

You're right. I don't know any of the intricate details of your life. However, God does, and he still forgives you. For some of you, it's time to forgive yourself and walk in victory in life.

When You're Down to Nothing, God Is Up to Something

It's difficult for us to discern how God is "working all things together for the good" when things continue to get worse. God began writing your life story in eternity past and is continuing to write to eternity future. Unfortunately, we are unable to see the finished product of God's handiwork of the tapestry of our lives. Little did I know when I decided to attend William Carey College in 1994 that God was working behind the scenes to bring me to a school where I would hear the gospel. Although I wasn't born again at that moment, I would remember that conversation with Jeremy Brown seven years later. After my car accident and drug addiction, my life spiraled out of control. Stealing from my parents and living without gas, electricity, and water humiliated me in many ways. But when we're down to nothing, God's up to something. A season of sobriety brought hope for the future, but a relapse took me back to ground zero again. Why is this happening to me? Would I ever get myself out of this mess? Little did I know, God was breaking me of all dependence upon self. The moment I relinquished control of my life once and for all, he stepped in and saved me. There are no accidents in God's economy. He's in full control of everything that happens.

You may wonder why God allows us to experience pain and suffering. I certainly pondered this notion. Every person mightily used in the Bible has endured some form of suffering. God's divine instrument for shaping us into the image of his Son is suffering. Author A. W. Tozer wrote, "It is doubtful whether God can bless a man greatly until he has hurt him deeply." At face value, his proposition catches us off guard. He offers an explanation to clarify his intention:

The flaming desire to be rid of every unholy thing and to put on the likeness of Christ at any cost is not often found among us. We expect to enter the everlasting kingdom of our Father and to sit down around the table with sages, saints and martyrs; and through the grace of God, maybe we shall; yes maybe we shall. But for the most of us it could prove at first an embarrassing experience. Ours might be the silence of the untried soldier in the presence of the battle-hardened heroes who have fought the fight and won the victory and who have scars to prove that they were present when the battle was joined.[4]

The first time I shared my testimony was at the Brantley center, a homeless shelter in New Orleans. Both my parents showed up to hear me preach, mainly out of curiosity to experience this new-found faith I was professing. After leaving the service, my dad, with good intentions, pulled me aside and dissuaded me from ever sharing my past again. He thought that since I was now changed by Christ there was no need to revisit past sins. I appreciated his concern for not idealizing my previous life; however, I felt as if God wanted me to share my testimony with others struggling with the same issues. Am I suggesting that you should glamorize or celebrate sins from the past? By no means. However, your story may be the connection point for someone struggling with similar struggles you've experienced victory over.

Remember, **God never wastes a hurt in our life.** He takes the mess we've made and redeems it in the form of a message we can share with others around us. He brings us through testing in life to give us a testimony. Our testimonies are evidence of the power of God in our lives. People may be able to debate Scripture with you or critique theological issues, but they can't argue with a changed life.

No One Is Beyond the Reach of God's Grace

Regardless of what you've done or who you've wronged, God can forgive you and redeem you. This motivates us never to stop praying for those who are far from God. His grace is greater than all our sin.

If we imagine God as a builder, then we, those whom he created in his image, are constantly under construction. God's always in a building project working on us. Paul emphasized this point in Philippians 1:6 when he said, "I am sure of this, that he who started a good work in you will carry it on to completion until the day of Christ Jesus."

Listen to the hope contained in these words. No matter how good it is now, no matter how terrible, no matter how far away from improvement you may feel, the final chapter of your life is yet to be written. God is still working on you, and the best is yet to come—it will be finished on the day of Christ Jesus. Since God wants to do so much with us, we have to be sure we are allowing him to do his work in us. It is dangerous to settle for mediocrity. I shared my testimony at our Celebrate Recovery ministry gathering one night and someone stopped me in the back afterward to comment on my message. He said, "I'm not who I used to be, I'm not who I want to be, but God's still working on me."

Don't give up on those whom you have been praying for. Extend the love of Christ the way God has showered you with it. Every one of us is in need of God's grace and mercy. Jerry Bridges said, "Our worst days are never so bad that you are beyond the reach of God's grace. And your best

God's Time is Not like our Time - a good example

days are never so good that you are beyond the need of God's grace."[5]

One Day at a Time

The best advice I can give you is be patient. You didn't get to where you are overnight, and God's not going to fix it immediately. Shortly after becoming a Christian, Brother Tim took our first discipleship group through a little book called *The Green Letters* by Miles Stanford. The words of his book that caused me to pause were these: "It seems that most believers have difficulty in realizing and facing up to the inexorable fact that God does not hurry in His development of our Christian life."[6] Later in his book, Stanford underscores the importance of patience: "A student asked the president of his school whether he could not take a shorter course than the one prescribed. 'Oh yes,' replied the President, 'but then it depends on what you want to be. When God wants to make an oak, He takes a hundred years, but when He wants to make a squash, He takes six months.'"[7]

Squash-like growth entice all of us because it's instant gratification. The results are immediate. The wait is short; the payoff is quick. However, God is never in a rush to do anything. In fact, the only time we see Him in a hurry is in Luke 15. When the prodigal son comes to his senses, the father (i.e., God) runs to embrace his repentant son.

Other than in isolated incidents, you will be hard-pressed to identify a time when God is in a rush. It took thirteen years before Joseph in Genesis was elevated to the right hand of the Pharaoh. If he had been released from prison when the cupbearer had promised, it is probable that he would have been sold to another Egyptian or to traveling traders. Without knowing the full story of Joseph's life, one would question the wisdom of God. But God had to press him, mold him, and shape him for thirteen years before he was courageous and accepted enough to stand before the reigning Pharaoh.

God's timing is best. There are certain lessons like patience, perseverance, and endurance that can only be learned through waiting upon the Lord. Life is much like a puzzle: we all have a handful of pieces, but someone took the box with the picture on the cover. We are left wondering how each piece fits with another. After an extended period of time, sometimes years, we pick up more pieces to the puzzle of life. Parts that once were disconnected start to fit into place. It is at this point that the image begins to take shape. As time goes on, we look back and realize that no pieces were wasted. Everything God gives us fits into the picture of our lives.

God uses every pressure, circumstance, and situation to shape and mold you into the man or woman he desires you to be. His choice weapon is pain. Pain reveals an area that needs to be addressed. It is in the crucible of adversity that character is forged. Think of the example of patience set by some of the founders of Christian faith:

- Noah endured mocking and humiliation for more than ninety years while he constructed the ark.
- Abraham waited for thirty years before God came through on his covenantal promise.
- Joseph endured isolation in a pit and incarceration in a prison before realizing the promise God made to him eleven years before.
- Moses wandered in the wilderness for four decades waiting to enter the land that was promised.

- Jesus waited thirty years before he began his earthly ministry.

Every day sober is another step toward usefulness in the kingdom of God. You may feel like you've missed out on so much because of wasted years, but don't be discouraged. Surrender daily to the Lord, depend upon his Spirit for strength, and watch him work.

NOTES FOR RECOVERERS

Completing this book makes for a bittersweet moment. I've just received word that Brandon, one of the friends I went back into the world to save, has passed away. The total number of friends I have lost since 2000 is fifteen.

These were not casual, distant acquaintances, but friends with whom I grew up, lived, partied, and had fun.

Brandon's death hits close to home. He was my size, my height, and my age. I might easily have been him, and he might have been me.

None of the friends I've lost set out to die prematurely. They were sons and brothers, nephews and husbands. Each had dreams and goals of changing the world as children. But somewhere along the way, drugs and alcohol controlled them.

No one sets out to waste his or her life. No one sets out to destroy himself or herself. But it happens every day—over and over. Somewhere a person dies from drug abuse every eleven minutes.[8] More people overdosed from drugs last year than died in the Vietnam War.

Very important for me

The issue of addiction is both physiological and spiritual. I'm not a medical doctor, so I won't delve into the neurological issues of dopamine and serotonin, although I have investigated my own genetic challenges. I can tell you, however, that the spiritual battle of drugs is very real too, and here are some lessons I've learned along the way:

1. Sobriety without Jesus Is a Dead-End Street

Addiction, at its core, is the sin of idolatry. When you think of idolatry, you may think of images of the golden calf in Exodus or carved statues perched on a shelf in someone's home. Those are indeed pictures of idolatry, but the meaning goes deeper. "The New Testament," according to *Eerdmans Bible Dictionary*, "extends the concept to include any ultimate confidence in something other than God."[9] Basically, anything we worship more than God is an idol.

The all-consuming focus of an addict is finding drugs—and not necessarily to get high. After a few months, the euphoric feeling isn't the same. There is the need simply to feel *normal*, or what normal has come to feel like. Friends called it "chasing the ghost."

Every morning I was consumed with one agonizing thought: *How can I score drugs?* Like most addicts, I would stop at nothing to get them. I wanted to stop, but I couldn't. I didn't know how.

The only person who can set us free from sin is the One who conquered sin, death, and hell: Jesus. The reason I went to rehab twice was because the first time I attempted to do it without Christ.

Sobriety without Jesus is a dead-end street.

NB

Γ Ξ

Think of addiction as a prison cell that detains you. Unless someone unlocks the cell door and sets you free, you're enslaved. You may experience seasons of sobriety or stints of abstinence, but long-term victory over an addiction is unattainable in our own power. And the reality is, even if I had managed to get sober without ever putting my faith in Christ, I would've been freed from one prison in this life only to enter into another in eternity.

If you have never acknowledged your sins before God and asked him to set you free, I want to encourage you to do that right now. When is the best time to ask for forgiveness from you sins? *Now.* There is nothing magical about the prayer you pray. What's important is the desire of your heart. When you realize you can't save yourself, and that Jesus is the only one who can, you will experience a new life in Christ. Sometimes it takes us getting so low that the only place to look is up to God.

But Jesus doesn't promise an easy life just because you're a Christian. We are still in a daily battle with the world, our fleshly desires, and the devil. Every day we must die to ourselves, our will, our desires, and our wants, and seek after God.

Jesus said, "If anyone wants to follow after me, let him deny himself, take up his cross daily, and follow me" (Luke 9:23). Long-term sobriety is not attained from the strength we have within, but from God. As Tim reminded me years ago in New Mexico, "The Christian life is either easy or impossible. It's impossible if you do it in your own strength. It becomes easier as you allow Christ to work in you to work through you."

My Fault

For me, every morning is a funeral and a coronation. I die to self and acknowledge Jesus as king of my life.

N·B

Very N.B.

2. Bad Company Corrupts Good Character

The longer you follow the Lord, the more you will cherish the words of the Bible.

Most Christians have life verses. These are verses that summarize their lives, have helped during a difficult time, or have provided much needed direction. This verse encapsulated all of those for me: "Bad company corrupts good character" (1 Cor. 15:33 NIV).

In other words, sinful people will corrode our values. And this is especially true for those of us with addictive or compulsive personalities.

You've heard the adage: "You are who you hang with." If that's the case, then we can determine our future by taking a photograph of our closest friends. I've told young people from time to time, "You can't soar with the eagles if you keep hanging with a bunch of turkeys."

When I experienced sobriety for the final time, I cut myself off completely from my past. If you want to experience victory, you have to ruthlessly eliminate anything that can harm you. Think of it as cancer. If your doctor diagnoses you with cancer tomorrow, would you say, "Let me think about removing it. I've had this skin for a long time. It's really not that bad." No! You'd remove it immediately. You'd cut it out. Why wouldn't you do that when it comes to your past life?

This doesn't mean that you should never spend time around unbelievers and seek to share the gospel with the lost. Of course you should. But for recovering addicts, you need to let other people be the ones to share the gospel with your old crowd. As my foolishness proved, it's unwise to think you're going to go back and share the gospel with your friends when you're a brand-new recovering addict.

You'll find yourself, like me, drinking margaritas and sharing the gospel before noon.

The first step you need to take is to get rid of your phone, change your number, and detach from your former friends. From experience in counseling people in recovery, I know this is the hardest step. For me, it was very difficult because I rationalized, "You don't understand. I lived with these people. I grew up with them. We partied together. We traveled together. We fought together. I can't just leave them."

All of those reasons were true; however, I was in no state to help anyone. I *needed* help. Distractions were my downfall. I was on a chair trying to pull people up out of the pit to be with me, but as with anyone standing on a chair, it's easier to pull someone off than pull someone up.

For three weeks, I had zero friends. I went from being the king of the club scene to king of nothing. I spent my days driving around town listening to Christian music and my nights reading the Bible. As I've described, my prayers were answered when Julie from college called me out of the blue to invite me to a Bible study led by T-Bone.

The rest is history. Trust that the Lord will bring people into your life to encourage, edify, and support you in his timing.

3. Stop Enabling

[This section is addressed to the relatives of an addict.]

If you trace the root of a perpetual drug problem, you can always find an enabler. Normally, it's the mother, wife, or husband of the addict. In my case, it was my dad. No parent sets out to contribute to the downfall and eventual death of a person. In their minds, they are helping them by paying for bills, providing money for gas, or giving them a place to stay with no strings attached. Love is the driving force behind the help; however, kindness, in this case, is seen as a weakness. And the addict will prey on that weakness to keep getting access to drugs.

During my addiction, I was a master manipulator, saying or doing anything to get money for drugs. "Robby, I thought you paid your cell phone bill two weeks ago."

"Sure, Dad, but this bill is for overcharges. I need it now—I can't wait."

Nothing got in the way of feeding the insatiable desire I had to get high.

Family members believe they are extending love by helping, but what they are doing is perpetuating the drug addiction. Addicts will never desire help unless they have hit rock bottom. You create a bottom for them by cutting them off, kicking them out, and not paying their bills.

I know this sounds harsh, but it's the only tactic for getting the attention of a person consumed with an addiction.

The reason this works is that addicts will always try to find another avenue to get high. When you cut off all roads, seeking help becomes the only choice.

When my parents kicked me out, it saved my life. It was the hardest three months of *their* lives, and they'll tell you that. But it was the best thing for me. I knew that I couldn't fix myself. Eventually I turned to Jesus.

Don't forget this: *If you keep being their savior, Jesus never can be.* Give them over to God and trust him.

4. Rehab Treatment

I have never seen anyone beat an addiction without going to some form of rehab. I've literally counseled hundreds of people over the last sixteen years—I get calls and emails each week—and I've yet to meet someone who has experienced long-term sobriety without going away for treatment.

Ideally a person needs to go away for a year, which is why programs like Teen Challenge work so well. The in-patient program teaches coping skills to those in recovery, while the body rejuvenates itself from drug abuse. Their success rate is higher than most treatment centers.

Most people, unfortunately, can't get away for that long a period. Another option is a three-to-six month in-patient treatment facility. I have sent many people to the Home of Grace in Van Cleave, Mississippi. Many of these centers exist. You will want to find a place that is biblically based.

The gold standard of treatment is where I went. Thankfully, the amino acid treatment is now approved in the States, so you won't have to stay ten days in Tijuana, Mexico. Paula Norris Mestayer and her husband Dr. Richard Mestayer run the Springfield Wellness Center in Springfield, Louisiana. Patients stay at the retreat center and receive a NAD drip for ten days.

As unbelievable as it sounds, the treatment from start to finish is complete in those ten days. Because NAD is found in every cell, the treatment minimized my withdrawals, reduced the body aches, and removed the cravings by the time I left. It feels like being one year into your sobriety when you leave the facility.

It's not cheap, but it's effective. I've sent dozens of people to Paula and have seen most of them experience sobriety by going through the treatment over the years. In addition to the treatment, Dr. Mestayer, Paula, and her staff provide counseling and support. If you can afford to go there, I would recommend it.

(For information on recovery help, check out our website: www.recoveredtreatment.com.)

5. Long-Term Care

Regardless of where you go for rehab treatment, the journey is not over when you return. That's where the hard work begins.

The temptation is to stop going to meetings, start hanging with old friends, and begin drinking socially—at least that's what I did the first time I relapsed. You didn't destroy your life overnight; it won't be fixed overnight. While the physical withdrawals from using may be diminished, the habits and desires that drove you to drug abuse are still lurking.

You will need to attend meetings for accountability and support. My counselor years ago suggested I attend ninety AA meetings in ninety days. After a few weeks, I was asked by the support group to stop talking about Jesus by name. That didn't deter me from going, but what did were the stories of people who never could experience long-term victory over sin. Week after week I heard people share defeated stories of hanging on and white-knuckling their sobriety.

I knew in my heart they didn't know the difference that made all the difference in the world: Jesus.

After Meeting 45, I stopped going. Instead, I engrossed myself in the church. Whenever the doors were open, I was there. Monday night visitation, I was there. Tuesday night

Bible study, I was there. Wednesday night prayer meeting, Friday night hangout time, Sunday morning worship, Sunday school, and Sunday night worship—I didn't miss a one.

Years later, I heard of a program that I wish I'd known about years before: Celebrate Recovery. John Baker took the structure of AA and reinstituted the Christ-centered principles that had been removed through the years. Using the Sermon on the Mount as a guide, he created a scriptural process for long-term sobriety.

I have offered Celebrate Recovery at every church I've pastored. Most Christians miss out on the benefits of this ministry because they think it's only for drug addicts, when in fact it offers help for sexual addiction, anger, physical/emotional abuse, and codependency. Parents or spouses who are enablers would benefit from attending a meeting with their family member. Since meetings are offered at different churches on different nights of the week, those in recovery can almost always find a meeting to fill their time.

N B

6. Read Your Bible Daily

Something I learned in my computer science class was, "Garbage In, Garbage Out." When useless information is inserted into a computer, garbage comes out.

The same can be said about our minds. For years, I polluted my mind with immoral images and ungodly experiences. The good news is that our lives can be transformed by the "renewing of [our] mind[s]" (Rom. 12:2). God promised to transform his people through his Word. If Jesus was the walking Word, as John states in John 1, we should get into the Word until the Word gets into us.

N.B

If you're like I was, you won't know where to begin. When I was a new Christian, I used the "OPRA" technique for reading the Bible: I would randomly *open* the Bible, *point* to a passage, *read* the verse, and try to figure out a way to *apply* it to my life. Thankfully, I didn't land on the Scripture that says, "He [speaking of Judas Iscariot] went and hanged himself" (Matt. 27:5)!

NB ᴦ Reading random Scripture verses will not provide solid biblical growth any more than eating random foods out of your pantry will provide solid physical growth. An effective reading plan is required.

My wife Kandi and I developed a reading plan called the Foundational 260. The F-260 is a two-hundred sixty-day reading plan that highlights the foundational passages of Scripture that every disciple should know. After failed attempts of reading through the Bible in a year with previous discipleship groups, I wanted a manageable plan that believers who have never read the Bible before could complete.

The plan asks believers to read one or two chapters a day for five days each week, with an allowance for weekends off. The two off-days a week are built in, so you can catch up on days where you're unable to read.

With a traditional reading plan of four to five chapters a day, unread chapters can begin to pile up, forcing us to skip entire sections to get back on schedule. It reduces Bible reading to a system of box-checking instead of a time to hear from God.

The amount of required reading also makes it difficult to sit and reflect on what you've read for that day. In order to digest more of the Word, the F-260 encourages believers to read less and to keep an H. E. A. R. journal.

And what's a H. E. A. R. journal? It's a journaling method that promotes reading the Bible with a life-transforming purpose. No longer will your focus be on checking off the boxes on your daily reading schedule; your purpose will instead be to read in order to understand and respond to God's Word. The acronym H. E. A. R. stands for Highlight, Explain, Apply, and Respond.

Each of these four steps contributes to creating an atmosphere to hear God speak. After settling on a reading plan and establishing a time for studying God's Word, you will be ready to H. E. A. R. from God.

As an illustration, let's assume you begin your quiet time in the book of 2 Timothy, and today's reading is the first chapter of the book. Before reading the text, pause to sincerely ask God to speak to you. It may seem trite, but it is absolutely imperative that we seek God's guidance in order to understand his Word (1 Cor. 2:12–14). Every time we open our Bibles, we should pray the simple prayer that David prayed: "Open my eyes, that I may behold wondrous things out of your law" (Ps. 119:18 ESV).

After praying for the Holy Spirit's guidance, open your notebook or journal, and at the top left-hand corner, write the letter H. This exercise will remind you to read with a purpose. In the course of your reading, one or two verses will usually stand out and speak to you. After reading the passage of Scripture, highlight each verse that speaks to you by copying it under the letter "H". Write out the following:

- The name of the book
- The passage of Scripture
- The chapter and verse numbers that especially speak to you
- A title to describe the passage

This practice will make it easier to find the passage when you want to revisit it in the future.

After you've highlighted the passage, write the letter "E" under the previous entry. At this stage you will *explain* what the text means. By asking some simple questions, with the help of God's Spirit, you can understand the meaning of a passage or verse. The next chapter will teach you in detail how to understand the meaning of a passage. Until then, here are a few questions to get you started:

- Why was this written?
- To whom was it originally written?
- How does it fit with the verses before and after it?
- Why did the Holy Spirit include this passage in the book?
- What is he intending to communicate through this text?

At this point, you are beginning the process of discovering the specific and personal word that God has for you from his Word. What is important is that you are engaging the text and wrestling with its meaning.

You may look at the questions above and think, *I wouldn't know where to start answering those.* There are several good resources, but I would recommend buying a good study Bible. I helped compile the *CSB Disciple's Study Bible,* and there are several good options, including the *CSB Study Bible, The New Inductive Study Bible* by Kay Arthur, the *ESV Study Bible,* the *ESV Gospel Transformation Study Bible,* and the *NIV Zondervan Study Bible.*

Use a resource like this to help you understand the Bible, but don't forget to do the hard work for yourself. Try to discover the answers on your own from your effort, and only consult the study Bible as a last resource.

After writing a short summary of what you think the text means, write the letter "A" below the letter "E". Under the "A", write the word *Apply*. This application is the heart of the process. Everything you have done so far culminates under this heading. After all, the Bible tells us to be doers of the Word, and not hearers only (James 1:22). As you have done before, answer a series of questions to uncover the significance of these verses to you personally, questions like:

- How can this help me?
- What does this truth mean for my life?
- What would the application of this verse look like in my life?
- What is God saying to me?
- How should this change me?

These questions bridge the gap between the ancient world and your world today. They provide a way for God to speak to you from the specific passage or verse. Answer these questions under the "A". Challenge yourself to write between two and five sentences about how the text applies to your life.

Finally, below the first three entries, write the letter "R" for *Respond*. Your response to the passage may take on many forms. You may write a call to action. You may describe how you will be different because of what God has said to you through his Word. You may indicate what you are going to do because of what you have learned. You may respond by writing out a prayer to God. For example, you may ask God to help you to be more loving, or to give you a desire to be more generous in your giving. Keep in mind that this is your response to what you have just read.

Notice that all of the words in the H. E. A. R. formula are action words: **H**ighlight, **E**xplain, **A**pply, and **R**espond. God does not want us to sit back and wait for him to drop some truth into our laps. Instead of waiting passively, God desires

N.B

7

that we actively pursue him. Jesus said, "Ask, and it will be given to you. Seek, and you will find. Knock, and the door will be opened to you" (Matt. 7:7).

Think of the miracle of the Bible. Over centuries of time, God supernaturally moved upon a number of men in an unusual way that resulted in them writing the exact words of God. God led his people to recognize these divine writings, and to distinguish them from everything else that has ever been written.

Then God guided his people to recognize the exact sixty-six books that were to be included in the Bible. The preservation and survival of the Bible is as miraculous as its writing. Then God gave men, beginning with Gutenberg's printing press, the technology to copy and transmit the Bible so that all people could have it. All because God has something to say to you.

Memorizing the Word

While many plans for memorizing Scripture are effective, a simple system has been effective for me. All you need is a pack of index cards and a committed desire to memorize God's Word. It's easy: write the reference of the verse on one side of the card and the text of the verse on the other. Focus on five verses at a time, and carry your pack of Scripture cards with you.

Throughout the day, whenever you have a few minutes, pull out your pack of Scripture cards and review them. Read the reference first, followed by the verse. Continue to recite the verse until you get a feel for the flow of the passage. When you are comfortable with the text, look only at the reference side of the card in order to test your recall.

It is important to recite the reference first, then the verse, and finish with the reference again. This will prevent you from becoming a "concordance cripple." As a new believer, I was forced to look up every verse in the concordance at the back of my Bible. Sometimes, when I quoted a Scripture while witnessing, the person would ask me, "Where did you get that?"

I could only respond, "Somewhere in the Bible." As you can imagine, that's less than effective when sharing with others! By memorizing the references, you will speak with authority and gain the respect of your hearers when you quote Scripture.

When you master five verses, begin to study five more. Review all the verses you have learned at least once a week. As your pack grows, you will be encouraged to keep going in Scripture memorization, and you will experience its powerful effects in your life.

(For disciple-making resources, check out our website: www.replicate.org.)

A Final Thought

People ask me all the time, "Would you ever have thought you would be married with two boys, an author, a doctor, and the pastor of a megachurch?"

Honestly, the person who is most amazed at what God has done over the years is *me*. I've witnessed firsthand every heartbreak, every situation, and every encounter.

The follow-up question usually is: "What's the secret to being used by God?"

My answer is simple: there are no secrets in the Christian life. The secrets are the obvious things: prayer, reading the

Word, and obeying the Lord. When I got saved, I made a deal with the Lord. Up to that point, I was pushing the envelope of drug abuse, so I couldn't lose in a sense, because I didn't want to live much longer anyway. "God," I offered, "if you save me, I will go after you with the same intensity I did to get high."

For those who know anything about addicts, you don't get in the way of someone trying to get high. I'd never forgotten what Paula told me years before about being a laser beam pointed in the wrong direction. I wondered, *What could happen if I go all in after God?*

Since the day I met Christ, I've never gotten over being saved. I think that was the apostle Paul's secret to ministry. He never became blasé or matter-of-fact about the reality that Christ saved him. As an old man, facing death by execution, he still wanted to shout it from the rooftops. He was saved!

Sadly, many Christians have forgotten that they were at one time living in darkness. We become institutionalized and domesticated when we forget about the moment we went from death to life.

Never let it be said that we got over being saved. God made us different to make a difference.

NOTES

1. C. S. Lewis, *The Screwtape Letters* (Cambridge: Samizdat Press, 1941; 2016), 24.

2. The doctor's name has been changed to protect her identity.

3. https://en.wikipedia.org/wiki/Islam_in_Indonesia

4. A. W. Tozer, *The Root of the Righteous* (Chicago, IL: Moody, 1955; 2015), 164.

5. Jerry Bridges, *The Discipline of Grace* (Colorado Springs, CO: NavPress, 1994).

6. Miles J. Stanford, *The Green Letters* (Grand Rapids, MI: Zondervan, 1975; 1983), 6.

7. Ibid.

8. https://opioids.thetruth.com/o/the-facts/fact-1005

9. Allen C. Myers, *The Eerdmans Bible Dictionary* (Grand Rapids, MI: Eerdmans, 1987), 512.

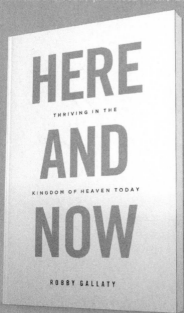

Rosies - plumber - Tuesday I
must phone 07860 833304

0330 123 9243

BQ abbey retail park.
What worries you, martens you

baking Powder
Eggs , Milk
- whole oat slices of bread
dip them in the Egg. Milk
baking powder, small sugar
Than deeps fry, Thick slices of
Bread

Disciplemaking resources to grow your people.

"An outstanding introduction to the basics of the faith
in a manner that will equip Christians to grow into maturity."

THOM S. RAINER

"I want to encourage you as clearly as I possibly
can. Please don't read this book. Instead, do it."

DAVID PLATT

"Read this book, be encouraged, and then pass it on to a fellow pilgrim."

RUSSELL D. MOORE

This Week I must do.

1) Power Wash - The yard
2) Paint Fench - The Wood Fence
3) Put up coat hanger in hall - coat hanger
4) go make appointment at Vet - for pink eyes nails
5) Also make appointment to have pink eyes worked
6) Sort out my guitars - tune them, change their cases, put one in the cupboards' & one in my corner, behind curtain, so that I can start playing it again more often to practise my songs & write new ones
7) Work on my bike, - wash it, oil all the parts with Q2 spray, chain, etc - Then paint all screws with black nail polish to cover the rust on them.
8) Phone the bycicle shop in Belfast to arrange what time I can take it there to have new tyres put on & a carrier on the back
9) Monday or some day next week go to town go to bank & pay my credit card
8) Sort out my HIFI & guitar amp